Seven Dark Rivers

and

The Salvation Army

Seven Dark Rivers and The Salvation Army

by John D. Waldron

© 1990 The Salvation Army, New York

ISBN: 0-89216-092-6

Published by: The Salvation Army Literary Department
(USA Eastern Territory)
145 West 15th Street
New York, N.Y. 10011

Printed in the United States of America

First Printing--1990

Cover art: Courtesy of The Salvation Army
Canada and Bermuda Territory

SEVEN DARK RIVERS

AND THE SALVATION ARMY

An Anthology of Salvationist Writings:

In celebration of the 100th anniversary of the publication of William Booth's epic volume on Christian philanthropy, *In Darkest England and the Way Out.*

In reflection of Booth's visions of human misery and despair, and on contemporary endeavors to fulfill his dreams with Christian compassion and dedicated skills.

Compiled by
John D. Waldron

Published by
The Salvation Army
(USA Eastern Territory)
Literary Department
145 West 15th Street
New York, N.Y. 10011

OTHER BOOKS BY THE SAME ANTHOLOGIST

At the Center of the Circle (Brengle)

The Privilege of All Believers

G. S. R. (Railton)

O Boundless Salvation

The Salvationist and the Atonement

Women in The Salvation Army

The Army Bookshelf

The Salvation Army and the Children

The Salvation Army and the Churches

Creed and Deed (Social Theology)

Pioneering Salvationists

The Salvationist and the Scriptures

Fan the FLAME (Finney)

The Salvationist Lifestyle

PREFACE BY THE COMPILER

When William Booth published his great manifesto, *In Darkest England and the Way Out*, the world was shocked by its stark realism, as Booth revealed the misery and depravity of the "submerged tenth" of England's population.

The evils against which The Salvation Army wages warfare one hundred years later are still loathsome, repulsive, and frightening (although they are frequently camouflaged with glitter and luminescence!). Your compiler often found the research to be depressing. However, the chapters are realistic pictures of life as it is--together with stories of the Army's healing ministry.

The Priest of the Jericho Road was not the first, or the last, "religious" person who found it more convenient to "pass by on the other side."

But that is not the Christlike response to human despair and degradation. It is not the Salvation Army way, or the way of Catherine and William Booth. Those who are called by His name are challenged to meet evil in all its forms, to render sacrificial service for His sake, and to respond to the challenge, "Inasmuch as you have done it unto one of the least of these My brethren, you have done it unto Me."

Read these chapters through the eyes of the One Who touched leprous flesh, and cast out vicious devils, and rescued a prodigal from the hogs, and wept over human despair and evil. Let your heart be moved as you reflect on the servanthood of Jesus, as depicted in Edward Read's penetrating hymn:

> The basin and the towel,
> And Jesus on his knees.
> What graciousness is here,
> What holy mysteries!
> How needs of mine assail me when
> I watch the Master and His men.
>
> The basin brims with grace,
> As Jesus comes again;
> He holds the towel to me
> To serve men in His name.
> To share such Christly ministries
> I can but fall upon my knees.

FOREWORD

"In war," said Winston Churchill, "armies must fight," and certainly The Salvation Army is no exception.

From our beginnings, we have recognized that we are called to an active and re-active role, set amid the hostile iniquities of a sinful world to seek with compassion but also to oppose with conviction all that drags human beings down into darkness.

In this book, yet another anthology compiled by Commissioner John Waldron (R), the salvation soldier is provided with weapons for warfare -- the considered comments and informed arguments of many spokesmen for the movement aware of dark currents of evil and describing their dangers and their destination.

It is my hope that many Salvationists will use this book as a resource in a continual war against evil.

Eva Burrows.

GENERAL

INTRODUCTION

In 1890, William Booth published his monumental epic on human misery and poverty, *In Darkest England and the Way Out*. Each page had been reviewed with the Army Mother, Catherine Booth. His dedication of the book to her marks it as a combined vision of the co-founders of The Salvation Army. Although she was "promoted to Glory" just days before it was published, her compassionate concern is absorbed into the Scheme propounded by the General.

The first edition of 10,000 was sold out on the first day, and it has been through many reprints, in many languages, since it burst upon England on October 20, 1890.

Within a decade, the "Social Wing" (the implementing arm of the Darkest England Scheme) had grown dramatically, with a bewildering network of related services throughout the world. Within two decades, hundreds of officers and employees were involved in scores of caring and philanthropic ministries, and it was felt advisable to bring these workers together from all parts of the world to hear the General describe the basic philosophy of Salvation Army social work.

These International Councils were convened by William Booth in 1911, the year before his death. His addresses-- vigorous, challenging, prophetic--have been preserved for us, and help us to identify the evils against which he was waging an unremitting warfare, and his battle plans for victory.

In an introductory lecture on "The Need," he shares his deep compassion and insight. Declaring that "this is perhaps the most important topic I have to bring before you," he describes, with vivid imagery, the "seven dark rivers" of evil.

To the assembled officers, he pours out his soul. "The world is crowded with misery. It seems to me as though you could, with a little imagination, discern seven dark rivers, each swollen with tears and stained with blood, and rolling with endless twists and turns through the vast populations that cover the surface of the earth."

He then identifies these rivers, and succeeding lectures describe them in detail, together with the Army's efforts to stem the tide. He names the rivers of:
Grinding Poverty
Disease
Lust
(The Unlawful Gratification of the Physical Appetites)
Crime
War (Including Fighting of Every Description)
Despair
Atheism.

"There they are," he exclaims, "these rivers, rolling through the world, each one of them bearing on its waters, wherever it may be found, any amount of misery and woe. There they are, the enemies of the race, the foes of God, and the forerunners of everlasting fire."

Even the most casual observer must agree that they are still flowing, "with endless twists and turns," through today's society. The number of "tributaries" has expanded dramatically, and the Army's ministries have taken creative new forms in response to Booth's charge to "either dry up these streams, to stop their flow on earth, or to rescue the sufferers."

He does not underestimate the dimensions of the task, nor do we. He declares, "This is a gigantic task, requiring herculean efforts. The most powerful minds, the most highly placed individuals, and the most scientific students of human misery have, alike in all ages and in all lands, struggled to deal with these rivers, and have striven very largely in vain."

But the Salvationist must not be discouraged, and "must not rest satisfied with anything short of what is calculated, in some measure at least, to destroy this misery."

How do we accomplish this end? "The surest, shortest, most economic, most effective course ... to combat this ocean of misery is by the salvation bought for mankind by the sacrifice of Jesus Christ ... to do what is calculated to lead to that end."

The articles included in the Anthology are selected from a very extensive body of literature on these subjects. They endeavor to show some of the ways the Army has striven, and still strives, to fulfill the vision of its Founders--not only in the "Darkest England" of 1890, but in the "Darkest America" or "Darkest World" of the 1990s.

John D. Waldron

AUTHORS INCLUDED

General Bramwell Booth
General Evangeline Booth
General William Booth
Commissioner Samuel Logan Brengle
Commissioner Henry Bullard
Timothy Clark
Lois Hoadley Dick
Dr. James Dobson
Barbara A. Exline
Major Jenty Fairbank
Lt. Colonel Henry Gariepy
Commissioner S. Carvosso Gauntlett
Colonel Edward Joy
Henry Maule
Commissioner Andrew S. Miller
Thomas F. G. Coates
Mrs. Vernon (Dorothy) Post
Kenneth Rice
Lt. Colonel Miriam Richards
Bob Scott
Major James Tackaberry
Lt. Colonel Bernard Watson
An Unnamed Prisoner

A Prefatory Word from William Booth
(from *Darkest England*)

To attempt to save the Lost, we must accept no limitations to human brotherhood. If the scheme which I set forth in these pages ... is not applicable to the Thief, the Harlot, the Drunkard, and the Sluggard, it may as well be dismissed without ceremony. As Christ came to call not the saints but sinners to repentance, so the New Message of Temporal Salvation, of salvation from pinching poverty, from rags and misery, must be offered to all. They may reject it, of course. But we who call ourselves by the name of Christ are not worthy to profess to be His disciples until we have set an open door before the least and worst of these who are now apparently imprisoned for life in a horrible dungeon of misery and despair.(page 44)

There is not one sinner in the world--no matter how degraded and dirty he may be--whom my people will not rejoice to take by the hand and pray with, and labor for, if thereby they can but snatch him as a brand from the burning.   (page 226)

Only God can create a mother. But society needs a great deal of mothering, much more than it gets. And as a child needs a mother to run to in its difficulties and troubles, so men and women, weary and worn in the battles of life, need someone to whom they can go when pressed down with a sense of wrongs suffered or done, knowing that their confidence will be preserved inviolate, and that their statements will be received with sympathy.   (page 227)

TABLE OF CONTENTS

I. **Grinding Poverty** 1

Introduction
The Destitute Poor and the Suffering Saints   Jenty Fairbank
Obscene Death   Henry Maule
The Children of the Lost   William Booth
Sweated Labor   S. Carvosso Gauntlett

II. **Disease** 23

Introduction
The Sick, O Lord ...   Bernard Watson
AIDS: Pastoral Guidelines   USA Eastern Territory
A Salvadorian Baby and Open-Heart Surgery   Timothy Clark
    Kenneth Rice
The Valiant Nurses   Miriam Richards
AIDS Ministry in Zambia   *The War Cry*
General Booth as Faith Healer   Thomas F. G. Coates

III. **Lust** (Unlawful Gratification of Physical Appetites) 65

Introduction
The Army's Social Revolution in Japan   Henry Bullard
The Pollution of Pornography   Henry Gariepy
    James Dobson
    Lois Hoadley Dick
    An Unnamed Prisoner
A Fight with the Dragon   Bramwell Booth

IV. **Crime** 101

Introduction
Criminals No More   Bernard Watson
The Salvation Army in Correctional Services   James Tackaberry
In French Convict Settlements   S. Carvosso Gauntlett

V. War (Fighting of Every Description) 135

    Introduction
    Disarmament   Evangeline Booth
    Doan Quan Cuu The   Barbara A. Exline
    World Disarmament and Peace   Andrew S. Miller

VI. Despair 167

    Introduction
    The Abandoned Child   S. Carvosso Gauntlett
    A Third Opinion   Bob Scott
    She Lights Candles   Dorothy Hughes Post

VII. Atheism 185

    Introduction
    A Rising Tide of Atheism   Samuel Logan Brengle
    The Power of the Name   Edward Joy

I. Grinding Poverty

From his world-wide travels, General Booth speaks of the poverty which he has observed "in every land to which I come."

He declares, "At the present moment, notwithstanding the improvements in trade, the increase of money, and consequently of food and other necessaries of life, the amount of abject poverty in existence is pitiable in the extreme."

He saw many of his people rising out of their poverty after a vital Christian experience motivated them to overcome the obstacles toward upward mobility. Booth declared: "Salvation will make him a satisfactory character, find him work, secure him friends, teach him thrift, ensure his happiness, and secure for him the guidance and blessing of his Heavenly Father."

Grinding Poverty (from *Darkest England*)

When long-continued destitution has been carried on to the bitter end, when piece by piece every article of domestic furniture has been sold or pawned, when all efforts to procure employment have failed, and when you have nothing left except the clothes in which you stand, then you can present yourself before the relieving officer and secure your lodging in the workhouse....

The stone-breaking test is monstrous. Half a ton of stone from any man in return for partially supplying the cravings of hunger is an outrage which, if we read of as having occurred in Russia or Siberia, would find Exeter Hall crowded with an indignant audience, and Hyde Park filled with strong oratory....

These tasks are expected from all comers, starved, ill-clad, half-fed creatures from the streets, foot-sore and worn out, and yet unless it is done, the alternative is the magistrate and the jail.   (pages 76-77)

Much has been said, and rightly said--it could not be said too strongly--concerning the disease-breeding, manhood-destroying character of many of the tenements in which the poor herd in our large cities. But there is a depth below that of the dweller in the slums. It is that of the dweller in the street, who has not even a lair in the slums which he can call his own. The houseless Out-of-Work is in one respect at least like Him of whom it was said, "Foxes have holes, and birds of the air have nests, but the Son of Man hath not where to lay His head.'(pages 32-33)

THE DESTITUTE POOR AND THE SUFFERING SAINTS

By Jenty Fairbank

From "Booth's Boots"

Published by
The Salvation Army
International Headquarters
London (1983)

A raw winter's day in the 1840s and an orphan--hungry, shivering, penniless--stood on London Bridge eyeing the comfortably-dressed, smug-looking man coming towards him.

"Spare us a copper, mister?" whined Boy Flawn. "I'm so 'ungry!"

"Get out, you little devil!" snarled the man of affairs impatiently.

The 10-year-old gazed after him, rage and hatred rising in his mind; above all swelled the sobbing vow, "When I'm a man, I'll see if I can't feed all the boys like me!"

Significantly, it was in the City of London's Pudding Lane (where began the Great Fire of 1666, and a stone's throw from that boyhood bridge) that James Flawn set up his vow in the form of a refreshment room. There, not only did he attempt to feed "all the boys like me," but he also catered for more specialized tastes. During the summer of 1865 and until the Booth family moved to Hackney in November, William Booth lunched on Sundays with Flawn at the refreshment room, Booth taking his own food and Flawn making him a cup of cocoa. After lunch Booth would rest on a sofa in a back room until it was time for him to return to the Mission.

Little indeed thought the cook-shop proprietor ... that in the future it should fall to his lot to use his business capacity and experience in pushing on a great salvation scheme, originating from the brain of that very man whom he curiously watched upon Mile End Waste.

"The cholera year, 1866, will never be forgotten by those of us who lived in London at the time," wrote George Scott Railton 20 years on, "... and the extremity of the East End misery had a great deal to do with many of the early arrangements in connection with the General's work."

In *The Revival* of January 31, 1867, William Booth writes that at the Union Temperance Hall, High Street, Poplar, "We are now giving away soup and bread, and propose doing so while the distress continues and funds are sent us."

The plight of the ship-building operatives was so dire that by mid-February Booth reported to *Christian World* the opening of an actual soup kitchen in Poplar, "supplying nearly 200 quarts of soup and a proportionate amount of bread per day."

The East London Christian Mission's acquisition of the one-time Eastern Star beer-shop at 188 (now 220) Whitechapel Road as its first headquarters in July 1867, and the fitting up of part of the premises as a soup kitchen, meant that by early 1870 "as many as two thousand poor fellows ... most of them paying pennies of their own" could be provided with soup in one day. Flawn's vow was already assuming impressive proportions.

And if there was an outcry, then as now, that nothing was given free, Railton had his answer: "Free breakfasts were given now and then on Sunday morning to people to whom tickets had been carefully distributed by men, once of their own class, who carefully hunted them out one by one until the tables were crowded with the poor, and maimed, and halt, and blind. But after soup and after breakfast came prayer, the prayer of men who meant to prevail, together with appeal upon appeal, urging to immediate surrender to God as the only remedy for their miseries, temporal and spiritual. Those prayers and appeals did prevail to the salvation of many," maintained Railton. Indeed, just a year later, *The Christian Mission Magazine* of February 1871 records that after a free Sunday morning breakfast for 500 of the poor, "men from the working classes address the listeners (one of them himself converted through a free breakfast two years ago at the theater)."

Before the end of the decade, however, Booth was to have second thoughts about the gratuitous handouts. "A free tea is certainly a method of gathering together many who could in no other way be induced to come and listen to the gospel of Christ. But we look with great doubt and little hope upon the crowds who come to seek the bread that perisheth, and who even when the Master himself dispensed it, generally went away unchanged spiritually."

Surveying it all stands Flawn, manager of this not inconsequential undertaking, working out his boyhood vow. Beside him works Bramwell Booth, eldest son of William; at 15 years of age, little more than a boy himself. Manager of four or five Food-for-the-Million shops, his role is to provide the poor with "Hot Soup Day or Night, Three-Course Dinners for 6d."

Meanwhile, *The East London Evangelist* of June 1, 1869, assures us, "The Sick Poor Visitation Society still pursues its quiet and unobtrusive way. In no more useful way can money be spent in relieving the poor than in visiting them when sick and dying. A little help is very welcome and ensures a quiet hearing for gospel truth," for from the earliest days of soup distribution all cases helped were visited and followed up. Prime mover in this vital ministry was Miss Jane Short who, having come under the influence of Catherine Booth's preaching at Margate in 1867, became not only a lodger in the Booth household and one of the Mission's district visitors, but "in addition had charge of the collection and distribution of old clothing and boots." Those boots were to become a recurring motif in the ever-evolving story of Salvation Army social work.

Jane Short's priorities were uncompromising. She it is who gives us one of the first clear statements of intent as far as the relationship between evangelism and good work is concerned. Writing in *The Christian Mission Magazine* of April 1870 she explains: "While the chief object and aim of The Christian Mission is to bring sinners to Jesus, we feel it a duty and privilege to minister to the bodily wants of the necessitous.... Parcels of old clothing, and old boots and shoes will be most gratefully received."

Clothes, boots, shoes--and now blankets. The Blanket Loan Society's ingenuity was to be outdone only by the introduction of maternal bags (this at Stockton in 1876); although at Whitechapel as early as 1869 "Mrs. Coates ... went to the mission hall for a box of clothes for the baby as a loan for a month." Meanwhile at Hammersmith teas were given for the oil-cake makers, the roadscrapers and the washerwomen.

Thrift clubs and mothers' meetings abounded, and of them Railton was later to write: "I should not like to investigate too closely the question as to how many stitches were put into the garments then in course of completion at those meetings, in any given hour. There is no doubt that many a poor mother was enabled, with the aid of a few pence carefully saved, to procure clothing, which would otherwise have cost many shillings. But in all the conversations I have had with those who made themselves generally useful in connection with these meetings, I have never once heard anything said about sewing. All their memories of the mothers' meetings relate to mother this and sister that, who, after a great deal of persuasion, were induced to come to such-and-such a meeting, where they got upon their knees and transformed into lovers of the Lord before they left the place."

"I can say religion is a good thing," testified the husband of one such woman at Poplar, "my body is stronger, my soul is saved, my wife is happier, my children are clothed, my house is better furnished, and, having signed the pledge and given over smoking, I can say, 'Godliness is profitable for all things'."

More succinctly, at Hanley some years later a convert claimed: "I had not any clothes when I got converted, but since I have joined the Army I have spent five pounds six on clothes in a few weeks. Glory to Jesus! And I'm saved in the bargain."

6

Socially elevating though salvation might be proving in some cases, Booth's rapidly expanding Mission found its steps increasingly directed towards the "destitute poor" who, through these ministrations, were fast being turned into "the suffering saints."

In a London reported in *The Revival* of 1874 as containing "100,000 winter tramps, 40,000 costers, 30,000 paupers in the unions, with a criminal class numbering 110,000," Booth might well assert, "Only Government can give effectual assistance," while regretting their lack of initiative in doing so. "The whole subject of poor relief is beset with great difficulties; but whatever controversies there may be as to the mode of its administration, there cannot be two opinions as to the duty of those who have wealth--specially those who name the name of Christ--to stretch forth a helping hand.... Ought we to allow our brothers and sisters in Christ to stand shivering at the relieving officer's door, to end their days in the union, or to be buried in a pauper's coffin? Let those who have wealth answer."

Those who had wealth continued to answer in ones and twos, never in very great numbers; but it was left to the visionary William Corbridge, Christian Mission evangelist at Hastings, to declare: "We shall become God's relieving officers."

Two years after the historic 1878 change of name from The Christian Mission to The Salvation Army, the first officer cadets were received for training. From all walks of life they came, but mostly from the laboring classes; small wonder that in a day when state grants were unheard of for any kind of education--let alone for such combat-style instruction as was the lot of salvation cadets--a standard advertisement for "clothing for the cadets" rapidly followed by an appeal for: "Two lads, active, godly, willing to make themselves generally useful. Good character indispensable. Only those accustomed to kitchen work need apply, by letter only, to J.F., Congress Hall, Clapton."

By this time he was known as "Commissary Flawn," the caterer for both training homes, Booth's mid-1870s policy decision to relinquish soup kitchens and food shops having freed Flawn for this equally essential work. If the war against sin was to be effective, then it must be thoroughly fuelled--on "Ten sacks of potatoes, from a friend, Thundersley, Essex; One barrel of apples, from Rector Rose; One sack of potatoes, from Mrs. Webb, Barnett; Two pecks of flour, from a friend; and Four bushels of peas, from Mr. Lawpard," if one acknowledgement of donation to training home supplies stands as typical fare.

Even so, Flawn's boyhood vow had yet to reach the height of its fulfillment. Was it Flawn's boyhood bridge Booth was being driven across late one bitter winter's night towards the end of 1887 when he became conscious for the first time of the niche-dwellers--men huddled in alcoves of the bridge, with only torn newspaper between their emaciated frames and the stone, the damp and the biting wind? Certainly it was Flawn's Food-for-the-Million manager, now in his early 30s, and The Salvation Army's Chief of the Staff, who was confronted the following morning by his hairbrush-waving father commanding: "Go and do something! We must do something." "What can we do?" "Get them a shelter!" "That will cost money." "Well, that is your affair! Something must be done. Get hold of a warehouse and warm it, and find something to cover them. But mind, Bramwell, no coddling!"

Within weeks that "something" was being described in *The War Cry* of January 21, 1888, as: "A New Departure. For some time now," the statement read, "the starving condition of great numbers of the London poor has appealed imploringly to us for help. Not only are there thousands who walk the streets of this great city with its palatial mansions, abounding wealth and costly luxury, not knowing where to find a meal of bread, but there are numbers more who have nowhere to lay their heads save in the shadow of the railway arches, in the recesses of the bridges, or in the seats in the public parks and squares.... We have now decided to do something towards alleviating this dreadful misery, and have taken large premises in the West India Road, Limehouse, in which we propose to establish a very cheap food depot, and also to furnish a sleeping shelter for the night."

Six hundred pounds was appealed for to launch the venture, with the pledge that even the smallest sums of money would be acknowledged in *The War Cry*--as indeed was: "6d. from A Sympathizer" and "1s. from Mrs. Eliza Brown." "A Useless Sympathizer" even managed ten shillings. At the formal opening of the "New Departure" in February, the offering, appropriately, was taken up in sugar basins.

The first "regulations" concerning the Food and Shelter Depot appeared in *The War Cry* of February 25, stating that: "packets of tickets for single meals or for lodging, supper, and breakfast, can be had for distribution by Christians not members of the Army, or by other organizations, although no Salvation Army officer will prevent the danger of 'charity' being the hindrance it too often is to ascertaining the genuineness of professed conversions. No one will come to our penitent forms for soup and coal any more than before!"

Writing of this "New Departure" some years later, Bramwell Booth explained: "Whole districts are occupied by sections of population who never can eat a decent meal--they try to live on bits and drops. Thousands of pounds a year are thrown away by the wretched system of

8

buying tea in decimals of an ounce, and coals in brown paper bags, and light by the farthing dip. To meet in some degree this need, the food depots were established.... Nor is this all. Large numbers of the poorest people earn a scanty livelihood by work which is done in their homes, that is, in the one, or at most, two rooms in which a whole family is brought up. Matchbox making, covering of tennis balls, artificial flower coloring, pulling the fur from rabbits skins, and various kinds of needlework, are among the trades so followed. In order to gain the merest subsistence in these occupations every moment of every hour must be put to the best advantage. So that, apart altogether from economical reasons, which always make fires a costly luxury, the preparation of food is looked upon as a nuisance, for the simple reason that it takes time, which should be used to increase the joint earnings of the whole family. As a result a custom of buying some food at minimum prices to this class was one consideration which let to the creation of our food depots." Flawn's Food-for-the-Million shops had simply been resurrected as the 19th-century forerunners of fast-food and take-away stores.

"Planted just outside the entrance to the docks," the Limehouse Food Depot provided--during the dock strike in the late summer of 1889--the focal point of the kind of relief work for which The Salvation Army has since become well known. "The huge strike of 120,000 of the most poorly paid, and fed, and clad, and housed, laborers in the world has ... produced upon the great metropolis an impression deeper than it has received for years past. The mere question of a penny per hour, more or less, has been completely over-shadowed by the larger question as to what this tremendous upheaval of the poorest may, any day, foreshadow. What changes in social arrangements might not the people bring about within a few weeks should they suddenly combine together, in their millions, to act, with one consent, resolutely, yet calmly, and without any breach of law?" *The Times* observed: "The Salvation Army are [*sic*] continuing to do a vast amount of work at their depot in the West India Dock Road, and it is the opinion of the leaders of the strike that had it not been for this place of relief the distress would have been much greater." *The London Daily News* went as far as to say that: "it has been impossible to move about in the neighborhood of the Docks lately without feeling one's self under a debt of obligation to them."

Two more food depots had been opened at Clerkenwell and Marylebone earlier in the year, but in the face of the dock strike emergency measures needed to be taken. The Whitechapel barracks were briefly used for this purpose (before being closed and altered into a regular food and shelter depot), as were Poplar barracks: and here, as at Limehouse, Canning Town and Stepney barracks, special religious meetings were held three times a day during the strike. "We have avoided, as usual, anything like mere charity doling," reported *The War*

Cry, "but have offered all meals at half the usual price.... In supplying meals at half-price we are naturally losing half the cost of each meal. It is gloriously remarkable to find our Australian forces quicker in coming to our help upon this occasion than the wealthy inhabitants of this country." Two hundred pounds had been sent by the Army in Melbourne for this purpose. "Mr. Flawn, the energetic and hard-working manager of the Limehouse Food and Shelter Depot, tells me that if the dock strike lasts much longer he will be finished. The place is simply besieged from morning till night."

Mr. Flawn, of course, was *not* finished. He thrived on all this hard work. With the launching of Booth's Darkest England Social Scheme in the early 1890s came more and more food and shelter depots, and descriptions of their openings are sprinkled with comments by "the universal provider, Mr. Flawn." At the end of 1893, when 3,886,896 meals had been provided that year, "Manager Flawn declares the removal of the Social Headquarters to 272 Whitechapel Road has had the effect of bringing to the counters of his food department hordes of the most miserable and wretched, the chilliest and hungriest human beings whom it has ever been his lot to encounter."

To his father in 1906 Bramwell Booth writes: "Flawn. Yes; he is living--very much so; he is in receipt of a pension, and shows no sign of dispensing with it! He will be most proud to see you." James Flawn "remained a keen Salvationist till his death at over 80 years of age in 1917." In that year alone 6,038,702 meals were supplied at Salvation Army cheap food depots in the United Kingdom. Could a 10-year-old, sobbing on London Bridge 70 years earlier, have imagined such an outcome to his vow?

OBSCENE DEATH

By Henry Maule

From "Moved with Compassion"

Published simultaneously by
Souvenir Press, London
and
Methuen Publications
Agincourt, Canada (1977)

The far distant dot against the diamond blue sky was, she knew, a vulture. It was poised prepared to drop like a stone at the right moment upon what it was watching far below it crawling upon the scabrous Indian earth. The right moment, which now could not be far away, would be when the skeletal Bengali child below was jerking in death throes. Already, great dark eyes blazing with fear in his skull-like head, the little boy was clutching agonisingly at his throat and choking, choking, choking.... He was in the ultimate stage of being eaten alive by hookworms and other intestinal parasites. They had devoured their way through his emaciated pot bellied body up from the soles of his feet and were now massed in their last obscene feast in his throat.

The very ground upon which the child was dying his horrible death was disgusting with the reason for it. The dank much trodden mud that gave onto the village tank (a rectangular artificial pond) was putrid with parasites and bacteria bringing many diseases and visibly writhing with hookworms. This diminutive worm (more technically the ankylostoma) enters the human body through the soles of the feet leaving a blister containing pus and accompanied by itching. From there they penetrate veins and rapidly squirm their way up to the lungs. Thence they escape successively into bronchial tubes, gullet and stomach. Within the duodenum and jejunum (the small gut) they attach themselves with their hooked teeth and suck blood, resulting in acute anaemia and, if untreated, death. Bengali children whose parents are invariably impoverished do not wear shoes or sandals. Playing as they do around the village tank, where the villagers do virtually everything, they are certain to have their frail bodies invaded by hookworms sooner or later. Other equally fatal worms enter through their mouths.

The woman who had chanced upon the death throes of the little boy was a white woman. She was Major Eva den Hartog, a Dutch officer serving with the International Salvation Army. In the scene that was now before her she saw the tragedy of the Bengali people. This doomed child, in a refugee camp at Barasat outside Calcutta, was only one small symptom of the people's agonies. There were other symptoms that were screamingly obvious at that very tank, traditionally a village's communal center. The static water was covered with a thick bright green slime that was almost a crust. In one place it had been broken by the zigzag entry of a woman to fill a brass drinking vessel. In another a woman wearing a sari was immersing herself as she took a bath, which the village women always did fully clothed. Further along yet another woman had scattered the emerald scum as she did the family's wash, wringing the foul water out of each garment before screwing it up to pound the moisture out of it on a flat stone beside her.

Even worse; not far away across the other side of the tank near a corner the dark figure of a Bengali man crouching beside a bankside tree. He was making no attempt to disguise what he was doing. He was defecating. And he was suffering from acute blood dysentery which meant that the foul excrement gushing from his pain-racked body was draining away his lifeblood and spreading more disease-ridden matter, inevitably into the waters of the tank. Even as this happened another Bengali woman, despite her crushing poverty regally statuesque with her brass pot upon her head, glided by the dysentery racked man on her way to the tank. From it she was going to draw drinking water for her family. What the man was doing was of no consequence to her because in her experience men always did such things just where they happened to be when the need overcame them; with virtually no facilities for sanitation there was nowhere else to go. In the street they did it, beside or on footpaths, beside the village tank, behind the nearest tree, anywhere. When guts were gripped by the agonizing pain of dysentery, or cholera, or even "simple" diarrhea, a man did what had to be done--and quick. It had been the same when East Pakistan, the land from which these people had fled, was the Eastern Bengal Province of India in the days of the British Raj. It seemed it would be like it for ever....

But impossible though it might seem that this ages-old Eastern problem would ever be solved, Major Eva den Hartog, from the clean, clinical West, was determined that it should. Just as determined as she was that the little child now ignored by his kinfolk in his death throes should not suffer the ultimate indignity of having his wasted corpse torn asunder by the poised vulture and its attendant carrion eaters. She knew what it meant, though she refrained from witnessing the obscenity herself. Within seconds of the watching bird spiralling down it would be joined around the child's body by others, like bald turkeys croaking with the voice of corruption, lolloping around in droop-winged anticipation. Then one would uncoil its long rubbery neck for its crimson cheeked face and jostle into the attack. Always the same procedure as the foul corpse eaters hobbled and flapped and gobbled, first a great beak up the anus to wrench out the entrails, then tear out the eyes, then whatever flesh there might be on the poor stark bones. Finally there would be the wrenching off of limbs and complete destruction....

That no such thing should happen to the child now before her was very clearly in the mind of Eva den Hartog. She stepped out across the fetid earth until she stood over the squirming child, a slight bespectacled woman of average height who might have been mistaken for a middle-aged ledger clerk, book-keeper or haberdashery assistant, were it not for the authoritative uptilt of her jaw at this moment. The very gleam of her spectacles was purposeful. Then, despite the fact that she was dressed in the crisp white tropical uniform of a Salvation Army nurse with a big

13

letter "S" on a crimson flash each side of her collar, she swept the poor befouled little mite up into her arms. Tenderly she carried him to where her colleague was waiting. "We must let him die in peace," she said to her companion. And when she did deliver the emaciated child to the emergency field hospital at Barasat, near Calcutta, which was there because she had willed it, Eva would certainly tell the attendant doctor: "You must let the poor little thing die quietly. He must be made comfortable so that he may die in peace." And she would be obeyed.

Although such instructions, which she had given before, were as humane as they were sensible, she had come under rebuke by one of the authorities in East Bengal for giving them. "Major Eva says 'Let the babies die'!" she had been accused, following a misunderstanding of an article in a British newspaper. But obsessed as she was with her mission to take healing and rescue to the stricken people in the disaster areas of the world, Eva den Hartog was in no way concerned by such an unjust rebuke. However, this did not mean she had become so hardened by the misery that she was arrogant under criticism. From the very depths of her heart she liked to quote, and often did, two favorite lines from a well loved and inspirational Salvation Army hymn:

Except I am moved with compassion
How dwelleth Thy Spirit in me?

Among the many disaster areas in which she had been heard to quote this, the very epitome of her belief, was at this refugee camp outside Calcutta. She had said it breathlessly when she first looked over the ocean of ragged tents and ramshackle shelters which spread before and beyond her, as far as the eye could see. They were the only homes of scores of thousands of men, women and children who until she came into their lives had been utterly without hope, any sort of hope, of anything at all....

THE CHILDREN OF THE LOST

By William Booth

From "In Darkest England and the Way Out"

Published by
The Salvation Army
Atlanta (1942)

Originally published by
The Salvation Army
International Headquarters
London (1890)

Whatever may be thought of the possibility of doing anything with the adults, it is universally admitted that there is hope for the children. "I regard the existing generation as lost," said a leading Liberal statesman. "Nothing can be done with the men and women who have grown up under the present demoralizing conditions. My only hope is that the children may have a better chance. Education will do much." But unfortunately the demoralizing circumstances of the children are not being improved--are, indeed, rather, in many respects, being made worse. The deterioration of our population in large towns is one of the most undisputed facts of social economics. The country is the breeding ground of healthy citizens. But for the constant influx of Countrydom, Cockneydom would long ere this have perished. But unfortunately the country is being depopulated. The towns, London especially, are being gorged with undigested and indigestible masses of labor, and, as result, the children suffer grievously.

The town-bred child is at a thousand disadvantages compared with his cousin in the country. But every year there are more town-bred children and fewer cousins in the country. To rear healthy children you want first a home; secondly, milk; thirdly, fresh air; and fourthly, exercise under the green trees and blue sky. All these things every country laborer's child possesses, or used to possess. For the shadow of the City life lies now upon the fields, and even in the remotest rural district the laborer who tends the cows is often denied the milk which his children need. The regular demand of the great towns forestalls the claims of the laboring kind. Tea and slops and beer take the place of milk, and the bone and sinew of the next generation are sapped from the cradle.

But the country child, if he has nothing but the skim milk, and only a little of that, has at least plenty of exercise in the fresh air. He has healthy human relations with his neighbors. He is looked after, and in some sort of fashion brought into contact with the life of the hall, the vicarage, and the farm. He lives a natural life amid the birds and trees and growing crops and the animals of the fields. He is not a mere human ant, crawling on the granite pavement of a great urban ants nest, with an unnaturally developed nervous system and a sickly constitution.

But it will be said, the child of today has the inestimable advantage of Education. No; he has not. Educated the children are not. They are pressed through "standards," which exact a certain acquaintance with A B C and pothooks and figures, but educated they are not in the sense of their development of their latent capacities so as to make them capable for the discharge of their duties in life. The new generation can read, no doubt. Otherwise, where would be the sale of "Sixteen String Jack," "Dick Turpin," and the like!

But take the girls. Who can pretend that the girls whom our schools are now turning out are half as well educated for the work of life as their grandmothers were at the same age? How many of all these mothers of the future know how to bake a loaf or wash their clothes? Except minding the baby--a task that cannot be evaded--what domestic training have they received to qualify them for being in the future the mothers of babies themselves?

And even the schooling, such as it is, at what an expense is it often imparted! The rakings of the human cesspool are brought into the school-room and mixed up with your children. Your little ones, who never heard a foul word and who are not only innocent, but ignorant, of all the horrors of vice and sin, sit for hours side by side with little ones whose parents are habitually drunk, and play with others whose ideas of merriment are gained from the familiar spectacle of the nightly debauch by which their mothers earn the family bread. It is good, no doubt, to learn the ABCs, but it is not so good that in acquiring these indispensable rudiments, your children should also acquire the vocabulary of the harlot and the corner boy.

I speak only of what I know, and of that which has been brought home to me as a matter of repeated complaint by my officers, when I say that the obscenity of the talk of many of the children of some of our public schools could hardly be outdone even in Sodom and Gomorrah. Childish innocence is very beautiful; but the bloom is soon destroyed, and it is a cruel awakening for a mother to discover that her tenderly natured boy, or her carefully guarded daughter, has been initiated by a companion into the mysteries of abomination that are concealed in the phrase--a house of ill-fame.

The home is largely destroyed where the mother follows the father into the factory, and where the hours of labor are so long that they have no time to see their children. The omnibus drivers of London, for instance, what time have they for discharging the daily duties of parentage to their little ones? How can a man who is on his omnibus from fourteen to sixteen hours a day have time to be a father to his children in any sense of the word? He has hardly a chance to see them except when they are asleep.

Even the Sabbath, that blessed institution which is one of the sheet anchors of human existence, is encroached upon. Many of the new industries which have been started or developed since I was a boy ignore man's need of one day's rest in seven. The railway, the post-office, the tramway all compel some of their employees to be content with less than the divinely appointed minimum of leisure. In the country, darkness restores the laboring father to his little ones. In the town, gas and the

17

electric lights enables the employer to rob the children of the whole of their father's waking hours, and in some cases he takes the mother's also. Under some of the conditions of modern industry, children are not so much born into a home as they are spawned into the world like fish, with the results which we see.

The decline of natural affection follows inevitably from the substitution of the fish relationship for that of the human. A father who never dandles his child on his knee cannot have a very keen sense of the responsibilities of paternity. In the rush and pressure of our competitive city life, thousands of men have not time to be fathers. Sires, yes; fathers, no. It will take a good deal of schoolmaster to make up for that change.

If this be the case, even with the children constantly employed, it can be imagined what kind of a home life is possessed by the children of the tramp, the odd jobber, the thief, and the harlot. For all these people have children, although they have no homes in which to rear them. Not a bird in all the woods or fields but prepares some kind of nest in which to hatch and rear its young, even if it be but a hole in the sand or a few crossed sticks in the bush. But how many young ones among our people are hatched before any nest is ready to receive them?

Think of the multitudes of children born in our workhouses, children of whom it may be said "they are conceived in sin and shapen in iniquity," and, as a punishment of the sins of the parents, branded from birth as bastards, worse than fatherless, homeless, and friendless, "dammed into an evil world," in which even those who have all the advantages of a good parentage and a careful training find it hard enough to make their way. Sometimes, it is true, the passionate love of the deserted mother for the child which has been the visible symbol and the terrible result of her undoing stands between the little one and all its enemies.

But think how often the mother regards the advent of her child with loathing and horror; how the discovery that she is about to become a mother affects her like a nightmare; and how nothing but the dread of the hangman's rope keeps her from strangling the babe on the very hour of its birth. What chances has such a child? And there are many such.

In a certain country that I will not name, there exists a scientifically arranged system of infanticide cloaked under the garb of philanthropy. Gigantic foundling establishments exist in its principal cities, where every comfort and scientific improvement is provided for the deserted children, with the result that the State assumes the responsibility.

We do something like that here, but our foundling asylums are the Street, the Workhouse, and the Grave. When an English Judge tells us, as Mr. Justice Wills did the other day, that there were any number of parents who would kill their children for a few pounds' insurance money, we can form some idea of the horrors of the existence into which many of the children of this highly favored land are ushered at their birth.

The overcrowded homes of the poor compel the children to witness everything. Sexual morality often comes to have no meaning to them. Incest is so familiar as hardly to call for remark. The bitter poverty of the poor compels them to leave their children half fed. There are few more grotesque pictures in the history of civilization than that of the compulsory attendance of children at school, faint with hunger because they had no breakfast, and not sure whether they would even secure a dry crust for dinner when their morning's quantum of education had been duly imparted.

Children thus hungered, thus housed, and thus left to grow up as best as they can without being fathered or mothered, are not, educate them as you will, exactly the most promising material for the making of the future citizens and rulers of the Empire.

What, then, is the ground for hope that if we leave things alone the new generation will be better than their elders? To me is seems that the truth is rather the other way. The lawlessness of our lads, the increased license of our girls, the general shiftlessness from the home-making point of view of the product of our factories and schools are far from reassuring. Our young people have never learned to obey. The fighting gangs of half-grown lads in Lisson Grove, and the scuttles of Manchester are ugly symptoms of a social condition that will not grow better by being let alone.

It is the home that has been destroyed, and with the home the home-like virtues. It is the dis-homed multitude, nomadic, hungry, that is rearing an undisciplined population, cursed from birth with hereditary weakness of body and hereditary faults of character. It is idle to hope to mend matters by taking the children and bundling them up in barracks. A child brought up in an institution is too often only half-human, having never known a mother's love and a father's care. To men and women who are without homes, children must be more or less of an incumbrance. Their advent is regarded with impatience, and often is averted by crime. The unwelcome little stranger is badly cared for, badly fed, and allowed every chance to die. Nothing is worth doing to increase his chances of living that does not reconstitute the home. But between us and that ideal how vast is the gulf! It will have to be bridged, however, if anything practical is to be done.

SWEATED LABOR

By S. Carvosso Gauntlett

From "Social Evils the Army has challenged"

Published by
Salvationist Publishing and Supplies
London (1946)

Some folk, it appears, collect match-boxes and their labels. A teacher of languages resident in London is said to have 15,000 different match-box labels--from all over the world: though the "queen" of this hobby evidently is a lady living in Surrey, whose collection is more than double as large: 35,000 labels!

Among this huge number, very probably is one bearing the crest of The Salvation Army, and inscribed:

LIGHTS IN DARKEST ENGLAND
Security from Fire --
Fair Wages for Fair Work.
The Salvation Army Social Wing.

To modern eyes the box would look rather large, perhaps clumsy; but behind it lies a story that is worth recalling.

About the time when William Booth's *In Darkest England and the Way Out* was published, the making of matches was a far from pleasant occupation. Wages were low--"sweated"--and working conditions dangerous. As in so many businesses, the welfare of the workers was scarcely considered, if only high profits and dividends could be secured. The matches were made in factories, where workers were paid on a piece-work basis, or in the poor people's "homes"--single-room tenements where men, women and children worked long hours, even on Sundays, to earn a few shillings.

Matches in those days were made with phosphorus, which had the advantage that you could strike them on any dry surface. But phosphorus was poisonous. If it got to the gums or jaw it caused necrosis--commonly called "phossy jaw"--which slowly ate away the jaw bones. This disease--also known as "match-maker's leprosy"--was most painful and, of course, disfiguring. Quite young girls suffered agonies from this "living death," and despite operations lost health and their occupation.

The most trouble arose, in the main, from the fact that the workers--most of them, it appears, women--ate without first washing their hands. Pay was so low that no time could be wasted, so folk worked on while they had their lunch or tea, and fingers dipped in phosphorus conveyed the poison to the mouth via the food taken.

Trade unions and others had protested, and various strikes had taken place. A number of people were striving to improve the terrible conditions. The Government issued regulations that factories must provide (a) hoods to protect the workers against the phosphorus fumes; (b) proper washing arrangements which must be used by workers before they partook of food.

That, of course, was an advance; but it did not effect very much until a model factory was established--an enterprise for which credit belongs to The Salvation Army.

In May 1891, the Founder himself opened this match factory, situated in Lamprell Street, Old Ford, London, E. It produced only safety matches, which did away with all danger from phosphorus. The premises were comfortable, light and well-aired. About a hundred workers were employed. A room was set apart for the convenience of those who wished to make tea.

The wages paid to match-box makers by the big firms was 2¼d. or 2½d. per gross. The Salvation Army paid its workers 4d. per gross. This, as the Founder said, was "a very considerable improvement," made possible partly by the elimination of needless "middlemen." A shilling, of course, was worth far more than nowadays.

Working at the average rate, a first-class box maker ... would earn 15s. a week as against, formerly, 9s. 4½d. A medium hand, producing twenty-five gross of boxes a week, earned 5s. 2½d. on the sweating scale, but would get 8s 4d. from The Salvation Army.

The selling price of these safety matches--not yet produced in vast quantities--was only slightly dearer than of those made with phosphorus by the large manufacturers.

Up and down the country the Army's venture found support--from the press, co-operatives and many business men. The chemistry professor at University College, London, spoke of the Army's matches as superior to others, and said: "We use these matches alone." The matches were being sold by the middle of 1891.

The great British match manufacturers soon had to abandon their old, unhealthy methods and conditions, and adopt better rates of wages. A firm abroad, using the process by which the Army made its matches, put on the British market boxes with the Founder's picture! The Salvationist enterprise had the desired effect, and by the beginning of the twentieth century safety matches were the rule, and "phossy jaw" was a matter of history.

The Army's factory was closed, and though this was but one venture in our battle for the rights of the poor, it is worthy of remembrance--next time you strike a match!

II. Disease

William Booth could not have envisioned, in 1911, the evolution of the Army's world-wide healing ministries. However, he reflected with compassion on the sick, perhaps remembering the months of dying agony suffered by his beloved Catherine.

He wrote, "Think of the crowded hospitals, the agonizing suffering, the gradual approach of the gloomy skeleton, and the reluctant partings and last farewells of kindred and loved ones, that are hourly taking place within their walls.

"In every neighborhood, and in almost every home, you find sickness, suffering, or death. Here is a source of constant anguish. I am not saying how far the sufferers themselves may be responsible or irresponsible for the painful conditions. I am merely reminding you of the sorrowful fact of their existence." The following articles give a brief account of the way Salvationists have endeavored to relieve this suffering.

Disease (from *Darkest England*)

Our officers were visiting one day when they saw a very dark staircase leading into a cellar, and thinking it possible that someone might be there they attempted to go down, and yet the staircase was so dark they thought it impossible for anyone to be there. However, they tried again and groped their way along in the dark for some time until at last they found the door and entered the room.

At first they could not discern anything because of the darkness. But after they got used to it they saw a filthy room. There was no fire in the grate, but the fireplace was heaped up with ashes, an accumulation of several weeks at least.

At one end of the room there was an old sack of rags and bones partly emptied upon the floor, from which there came a most unpleasant odor. At the other end lay an old man very ill. The apology for a bed on which he lay was filthy and had neither sheets nor blankets. His covering consisted of old rags. His poor wife, who attended on him, appeared to be a stranger to soap and water.

These Slum Sisters nursed the old people, and on one occasion undertook to do their washing, and they brought it home for this purpose, but it was so infested with vermin that they did not know how to wash it. Their landlady, who happened to see them, forbade them ever to bring such stuff there anymore. The old man, when well enough, worked at his trade, which was tailoring. (page 174)

I have been thinking that if a little Van, drawn by a pony, could be fitted up with what is ordinarily required by the sick and dying, and trot around amongst these abodes of desolation, with a couple of nurses trained for the business, it might be of immense service, without being very costly. They could have a few simple instruments, so as to draw a tooth or lance an abscess, and what was absolutely requisite for simple surgical procedures. A little oil stove for hot water to prepare a poultice, or a hot foment, or a soap wash, and a number of other necessaries for nursing, could be carried with ease. (page 179)

THE SICK, O LORD ...

By Bernard Watson

From "A Hundred Years War"

Published by
Hodder and Stoughton
London (1964)

There are two main groups of hospitals operated by The Salvation Army. First the missionary hospitals. They number about seventy-five, though a few are hardly more than clinics. Some specialize in one ailment, such as leprosy, tuberculosis, bone, skin or eye diseases.

They are found in Africa, India, Indonesia, Malaysia, Korea, Mexico, the Philippines, South America and the West Indies.

These cost about £500,000 a year to maintain, though much of the money is forthcoming from patients' fees and Government grants. More money must be found for them each year for the cost of healing rises alarmingly and they are a heavy drain upon Army finances.

As one might expect, the Salvationist hospital service of India makes up by far the largest item in this expenditure. Treatment of tuberculosis and leprosy, with aid for the victims of malnutrition, the high incidence of eye diseases and other maladies, call for more men, women and money than is available. Scurvy, rickets, beri-beri and pellagra are all endemic. These are, of course, deficiency diseases.

Secondly, the community service hospitals. These accept private patients and are the kind of hospitals that can render traditional Salvation Army services yet finance themselves.

These "commercial" hospitals sometimes make a Salvationist frown at what seems to be merely provision for the well-to-do. But the hospitals were founded in less affluent times, when poverty was widespread and efficient medical services in short supply. Apart from this the paying patient also "has a soul" as old-timers would have put it. The very poor and the comfortably off should all come alike to the Salvationist.

By far the largest group of public service hospitals [in 1964] is located throughout the United States where they are usually named Booth Memorial Hospitals. The large unit at Flushing, New York, is a noteworthy example of this kind of Salvationist medical center.

The Grace chain of hospitals in Canada are next in size [eleven in 1990]. They are large, well-equipped and utilized by the average citizens of prosperous townships. The new hospital at Winnipeg rivals Flushing hospital for cost and modernity. It would be considered a tremendous asset in any community in any country.

There are numerous general, or general plus maternity hospitals in Australia, South Africa, Switzerland, France, Sweden, Japan and elsewhere. Many of these, as in the United States and Canada, have separate wings or annexes for maternal service to unwed mothers. In that case there will probably be, more or less adjacent, a home or hostel where the women or teenage girls will spend some four to five months in the Army's care before the child is born.

The Salvation Army's tradition of hospital service, to a great extent, owes its existence to the "rescue" work, as such efforts for unwed women were termed years ago. From it, also, stemmed the Army's many homes for infants and older children, for it was often found that the baby born in the Army hospital became the Army's baby in a long-term sense, adoption being not then so conveniently arranged. To this day, in some countries, it is not uncommon for the mother to abscond, leaving the Army to hold the baby.

Nursing is probably the woman Salvationist's first choice of profession; many Army women make it their life's vocation and it goes without saying that the common-sense variety of religion motivating such devotion usually makes for good nurses. A like disposition to medical missionary work for men is not so widespread, probably because a doctor's qualifications are much harder to achieve.

The famine of doctors, created by the lack of sufficient young and qualified men and women Salvationists, has in the past been aggravated by serious losses for, as one might expect, tension is apt to rise between rather strict Salvation Army discipline and the ethos of the medical profession.

As a rule, doctors insist on managing their own affairs: the Disciplinary Committee of the British Medical Council, for example, deals with erring doctors of the British Medical Association. Similar professional "closed shops" exist in most countries. The Salvation Army Colonel or Commissioner is apt to look at things quite differently from the way the scientifically-trained doctor will look at it. The blind, unquestioning obedience of the zealous Salvationist, oft sung about in a phrase such as "My all is on the altar," comes not so readily to the medical man, at least with regard to his profession. For him the operative word may be not with the General, the Chief-of-the-Staff, or the Territorial Commander, but in the learned journals of the British Medical Association, the American Medical Association, and other medical publications.

But the Army is always willing to learn. Anxious to help its officer doctors, the Army has now established a Medical Missionary Section at I.H.Q., in London. The Salvation Army officer-doctor in charge co-ordinates the world-wide work, concerns himself with the recruitment of medical reinforcements, tries to find essential new equipment and supplies.

In the past, the anxiety of a doctor not to become out-of-date has been given insufficient weight in the Army. Any doctor worth the name needs refresher courses, time for extended leave to work under a specialist or to study and work for a further qualification. The medical liaison man in London, highly-qualified himself, sees the validity of this wish of any good doctor to keep abreast with developments in surgery and medicine.

Lack of men is the great problem. New steps are being taken to counter it. The Army is now showing an increased disposition to allow non-officer doctors, even non-Salvationists, to serve for one, two, or three or more years. In the past it has been assumed that officers alone could have the full sense of vocation and devotion required for such self-sacrificial toil. Already there is evidence that this is not so. The enlistment of specialist non-Salvationists is even more a startling idea in which The Salvation Army in Japan played a pioneer role. There is no doubt that the ecumenical movement, the thinner walls between various denominations, had made it less difficult for a non-Salvationist to work happily in a Salvationist team. So the idea is gaining ground that a Salvationist who is not an officer can be "called" to special work for God. And that someone not a Salvationist can have Christian faith and zeal at least equal to the Salvationist. These are great victories indeed along the "New Frontier" of The Salvation Army.

Wherever it is, of whatever kind, if the hospital is operated by The Salvation Army then the motivation will be the same as that enshrined in the hymn:

> At even, ere the sun was set,
> The sick, O Lord, around Thee lay;
> O in what divers pains they met!
> O with what joy they went away!

AIDS--PASTORAL GUIDELINES

From: "The Salvation Army and AIDS--Guidelines, Programs, and Services."

Published by
The Salvation Army
USA Eastern Territory
New York (April 1988)

Pastoral Care

The pastoral care of a person with AIDS is identical to that provided for a person with any other disease. This care may be given by The Salvation Army or by a spiritual advisor of the patient's faith. The person providing pastoral care must be sensitive to the needs of the family and of associates. There must be complete acceptance of the person with AIDS, without regard to his or her past personal behavior.

1. The Christian response to people with AIDS should be informed, accepting, nonjudgmental and compassionate.

2. The opportunity to talk with the patient, with family, and with associates about the spiritual dimension of life should be taken. The need of all persons for repentance, forgiveness, and the assurance of salvation should be sensitively broached.

3. The cultural values of the society in which the person lives largely color attitudes to death. Because AIDS is invariably fatal, the fear of death may well be an important aspect of the person's experience in dealing with the disease. Along with the fear may be guilt, a feeling of unworthiness, of overwhelming concern for family and friends. Pastoral care should include the witness to the faith, that there is acceptance and understanding through believing in Jesus Christ.

4. Pastoral care should include helping the person with AIDS inform the family and associates about the diagnosis and the care needed. It could be important for both the person with AIDS and the family and associates to have this contact.

5. Relatives and associates of persons with AIDS react in a variety of ways. Some may be embarrassed when they learn the diagnosis. Some may be angry. Some may reject and condemn. They may each require pastoral support. A simple explanation and the example of acceptance of the ill person can be helpful, also acceptance of validity of their present feelings.

6. As with all pastoral care, confidentiality should be absolute and the person's desire for privacy respected.

7. Martialling needed community resources and being part of the network of support services is also part of pastoral care.

Community Services

Persons with AIDS need a variety of services for their care and to help them maintain a quality of life that allows them to live with AIDS and to die with dignity. The Army should be part of the network that provides such services and should press the community to fill obvious gaps.

1. Each person with AIDS needs a place to live.

2. Persons with AIDS must have health care that is appropriate to the phase of the illness: out patient, home health aid, hospice, hospital.

3. Financial resources must be identified and used, including entitlements and insurance.

4. Legal advice should be available to help a person with AIDS organize his or her personal business affairs, including making a will.

Salvation Army Principles in Prevention

The present and growing number of persons with AIDS is found in the population that does not observe safe sexual behavior, and that shares contaminated I.V. drug needles. To prevent the spread of AIDS, the Army believes that:

1. The most effective method of prevention of AIDS is adherence to a life-style that includes premarital chastity, fidelity within marriage and abstinence from the use of harmful drugs.

2. Blood transfusions, and blood products should be used only from screened blood.

3. Discussion of human sexuality and sex education should be encouraged within the context of the family. Factual information about AIDS and the methods of transmission should be a part of this discussion.

4. Age appropriate education programs regarding AIDS, human sexuality and values including premarital chastity and fidelity within marriage should be developed for and used by all program areas of The Salvation Army: Corps, residences, and community programs.

5. An education program regarding substance abuse and the relationship to the transmission of AIDS should be developed and used throughout Salvation Army programs and services.

6. The Army should encourage the development of drug rehabilitation programs.

7. Because many participants in Salvation Army programs have already chosen behaviors that place them at risk, information about preventive measures including the use of condoms, sexual exclusiveness, and refusal to share I.V. drug needles should be available. The challenge is to hold fast to Salvation Army principles and at the same time to prevent the further spread of AIDS.

Education Programs

Misconceptions abound concerning the topic of AIDS. The answer to misinformation is always information and education. The Salvation Army administration recommends disseminating information about AIDS throughout all Army units. Suggestions for educational efforts include:

1. Encourage local Army units to secure information regarding AIDS, from hospitals, state and local health and social service departments, the media, libraries, and others.

2. Hold annual in-service training for staff/soldiers/volunteers/clients concerning AIDS.

3. Encourage local Army units to become knowledgeable of local community resources for persons with AIDS.

4. Obtain educational pamphlets regarding such issues as pastoral care, psychological and emotional complications, Bill of Rights for AIDS patients, written materials concerning human relations, dilemmas of people with AIDS, their fears, anxieties, hopes. A spiritual ministry can be enhanced by having such understanding.

5. Hold in-service training during officers' councils on the ramifications of the AIDS guidelines.

6. Post and adhere to hygiene guidelines in Salvation Army facilities.

A SALVADORIAN BABY AND OPEN-HEART SURGERY

By Timothy Clark and Kenneth Rice

From "GOOD NEWS"

Published by
The Salvation Army
USA Eastern Territory
New York (March 1988)

The phone call came to divisional headquarters in New Jersey like many other calls received during the holidays asking for assistance. It came from a gentleman in Maine, Glenn Baxter, Network Manager of the International Amateur Radio Network (IARN), a network of 700 ham radio operators in 40 countries. He had a special request to make of the New Jersey Division.

Jose Torres, a 2½-year-old boy from El Salvador, was in need of heart surgery. Without this surgery, available only in the United States, he would die. The Deborah Heart and Lung Center in Browns Mills, N.J., had agreed to do the necessary surgery free of charge through its "Children of the World" program if Jose could get to the Center, and the IARN had arranged for the child and his parents to travel to New Jersey. The hospital would provide a room and food for Jose's mother; but the IARN needed The Salvation Army to house and feed Jose's father, and to provide transportation for the Torres family to and from the hospital.

The IARN and The Salvation Army had crossed paths before. Members of the IARN had opened communications for the Army's medical team sent to aid victims of the Mexico City earthquake a few years before. They had also helped the Army during the San Salvador earthquake.

Divisional Commander Major William A. Bamford was quick to respond. Captain Pamela Findlay, a field representative for the division, was assigned to pick up the Torres family at Newark International Airport and take them to the Deborah Heart and Lung Center. Major Richard Shaffstall of the Montclair Corps, fluent in Spanish because of his service in Argentina and Puerto Rico, was to go along as translator.

The Torres family did not know who was to meet them at the airport or how they were to get to the hospital, but when they saw the Salvation Army uniform, they were immediately reassured--they were being met by fellow Christians. Their fears of the unknown faded quickly as they heard Major Shaffstall speaking their mother tongue. Even little Jose, as frail and small as a nine-month-old, perked up when he heard the Spanish--and when he was handed a stuffed toy.

The hospital conducted tests to confirm the preliminary diagnosis done in El Salvador, and found that Jose's heart had many different malformations, such as holes, blockages and enlargements. Surgery was scheduled without delay. Though it will probably be necessary for Jose to have additional surgery in the future, the immediate procedures were completely successful. The Torres family's trip home was made as easy
as possible. A Salvation Army officer met them in Miami and made sure they had no problems making their connecting flight back to El Salvador.

All of the events, from the IARN's first contact with the Army to the Torres family's return home, had taken only two weeks. "It's amazing what can be done when people work together," says Major Bamford. "The IARN, Deborah Hospital and The Salvation Army hope to be able to sponsor a child this way each year."

"When you think of how this all came together," says Glenn Baxter, "a ham operator in El Salvador calls the network in Maine about this child needing surgery. I call Major Mervin Morelock on the West Coast and he gives the name of the commander in New Jersey who says 'Sure, we can help.' The family flies to the U.S., doesn't speak any English, gets driven to Deborah Hospital, tests and surgery are done, it's successful and they are back home with their other two daughters before Christmas. All this in a little over two weeks time. It's mindboggling!"

THE VALIANT NURSES

By Miriam Richards

From "It Began with Andrews"

Published by
The Salvation Army
Salvationist Publishing and Supplies
London (1971)

Where can one begin--or end--the story of the valiant nurses who have so competently and selflessly backed up The Salvation Army missionary doctors? One solves the first problem by "beginning at the beginning," and paying tribute to the wife of Harry Andrews who bravely aligned herself alongside her husband to help in his devoted work for the poor and suffering around them in India. Earlier, while serving as a young officer with her sister in Poona, she had bravely given practical assistance to British troops in health safety measures when the city was plague-stricken. Wearing special clothing, she had helped the soldiers to carry out the sick and dying from their homes, afterwards heaping refuse from the sufferers' rooms into great piles and setting it ablaze. She had then shown the householders how to limewash their walls and disinfect their floors.

Quite untrained in nursing skills at first, Mrs. Andrews, after her marriage, learned from her husband how to bathe and dress a wound, and how to assist him at the scene of many an emergency operation, as well as in routine procedures, though it was only during the leave when Andrews qualified as a doctor, in 1919, that his wife received any specific training herself.

Mrs. Colonel Percy Turner was the first registered nurse to function in such capacity at the Catherine Booth Hospital, South India, which her husband founded. She had trained at Maidstone, England, where she had been a nursing sister, and had proved her capacity in Salvation Army women's social services at The Nest--a children's home in London--and at Ivy House, "the first Salvation Army hospital," opened in Hackney for maternity work and the training of mid-wives, and the precursor of the Salvation Army Mothers' Hospital at Clapton.

She travelled to India to become the wife of the "Catherine Booth's" first qualified medical officer, determined to give of her best to the cause her partner had so whole-heartedly made his own. From the first she assisted her husband in the hospital work with vigor, and it is recorded that "the birth of two sons and a daughter did not cool her ardor." The pattern of training Indian personnel in nursing was soon established, and the hospital became "a school of nursing issuing its own certificates and conducting its own examinations."

A somewhat startling pen-picture of this redoubtable pioneer appears in a description of Dr. and Mrs. William Noble's welcome to the Catherine Booth Hospital in 1921, at a time when Dr. and Mrs. Turner were nearing the end of their service in India: "Mrs. Turner, a rather stern-looking woman, stood nearby under a large open umbrella, an article she invariably carried, come sunshine or rain." But, if the Doctor Ammal (Mrs. Turner) looked, there is no doubt of the love she was able to inspire in her Indian comrades. "My dear Dr. and Dr. Ammal," one of them had written, in welcoming the doctor and his wife back from homeland furlough in 1919, "My wife and myself sincerely feel glad to hear of your long-expected safe arrival in Nagercoil.... We have been simply longing to see you both once more in this land which is so very dear to your hearts.... We have been praying with all our hearts to our heavenly Father to keep you from every danger and be pleased to bring you back to us in safety.... May God bless you both, and the dear children you have left behind in your homeland. Our many, many head-bowed *namaskarams* (the graceful 'palms together' welcoming salutation of the Indian) to you both."

Mrs. Turner was superintendent of nurses at the time of the Nobles' arrival. "There were eight trained nurses on the staff, three of them Indian. Captain Mabel Poole, one of the trained nurses, had studied tropical medicine in England. She had come to Nagercoil in 1919, was the pharmacist at the hospital, and when necessary served as midwife."

"From its early beginnings the Catherine Booth Hospital had a unique reputation for good nursing. At first many of the nurses had only practical training, plus such lectures and instruction in the wards and operating rooms as on overworked staff of doctors could provide them from time to time. Nonetheless, both Indian and European patients knew that when they arrived at the Catherine Booth Hospital they would get proper medical and surgical attention, plus excellent and attentive nursing care."

Mabel Poole, a native of Minehead, England, was training as an officer pupil-midwife at the Mother's Hospital, Clapton, London, during the First World War when she heard Dr. Percy Turner, who was on homeland furlough from India and was attached to the panel of lectures and consulting surgeons at the hospital, give a talk to the nurses about the land from which he had just returned and speak of his hopes for the future. The doctor asked for three volunteers who would "tend Indian patients, win their confidence when they were uncertain of the wisdom of contacting a Christian place of healing, and apply their knowledge of medicine and the message of the gospel."

When the Matron suggested to Captain Poole that she could render acceptable service in India, therefore, she was "not wholly unprepared." An interview with Dr. Turner followed and the young woman committed her life for service overseas. When her studies at the hospital ended she took a course in tropical medicine and in 1919 sailed for Bombay, arriving finally at the Catherine Booth Hospital. There, given the Indian name of Nesammal (Sister of Love), she began the tireless and adaptable service which was to take her not only to several branch hospitals, and the beginnings of leprosy nursing at Puthencruz, but also to include periods in the palace of the Maharajah of Travancore, the local potentate, on more than one occasion--once with the special charge of a very sick child of the reigning family.

When, after homeland furlough in 1927, Nesammal returned to India, she was appointed Matron of the Catherine Booth Hospital, a post she held for eleven years. "Her duties were little different from those of her earlier days at the hospital, though the buildings were larger and the staff increased in number." It has been recorded of her by a colleague that she had "amazing skill in complicated maternity cases" and that "her very touch seemed to bring healing."

Following a second period of service in the royal household, Nesammal was appointed in charge of the colony for leprosy sufferers at Puthencruz, in which she had a special interest, and despite a term of missionary service which was lengthened from the usual seven years to twelve years, because of the outbreak of the Second World War, Mabel Poole's years at the colony were not without happiness. A number of conversions were registered at the corps at Puthencruz and patients became Salvationists. In 1944 came transfer to Koratty, a government colony in the Cochin State run by The Salvation Army, where the Superintendent had charge of 420 leprosy patients--men, women, boys, and girls. She "possessed adaptability to a marked degree," supervising the growing of grain, root and fruit crops, and learning "something about electricity, motor cars, building, catering and water supplies." It was from this center that, in 1952 as a Brigadier, she retired from active service, to return to her aging parents in Watchet, Somerset, and to "continue a life of sacrificial service, seasoned by joyous adventure and motivated by daring abandon to God's will."

One of the number who was "trained on the ground" at the "C.B.H." was Brigadier Anna Lautala, who was appointed straight to the hospital from her native Finland, and arrived with little knowledge of even the English language. Very quickly she had gained a good working knowledge of English, as well as the Tamil language, and she soon became a byword for her skill and dependability. Doctors testified that she was "a tremendously valuable assistant" in the operating theater. Following her promotion to Glory, in 1969, the Indian *War Cry* carried a deeply moving tribute to her written by Mrs. Major Grace Sughanatham, the present out-patient sister at the Catherine Booth Hospital, whose husband is Superintendent of Nurses at the same establishment:

"Brigadier Lautala, widely known and remembered as Retnamoni Ammal, came to India as a missionary in the year 1921. Born in Finland, she was brought up by Lutheran parents but was later attracted to The Salvation Army.

"As a youngster, I had the opportunity of knowing the Brigadier while she was working with my parents in various branch hospitals. She was more than a family member to us. She was a hard worker and was loved by the local people for her untiring efforts in serving God. But it is the fellowship we had with her for which I remember her most.

"Again, when I became an officer I had the opportunity of working with the Brigadier in the Catherine Booth Hospital for many years, both in the theater and in the Eye Block. Retnamoni Ammal was a fully dedicated officer who loved the people who came under her care and moved very closely with them. Much of the Indian way of life was adopted by her, which helped endear her to those she served. She was quick to learn Tamil and was easily understood by all the patients and staff. In those days there were not modern facilities such as we have now in the hospital. Even the most back-breaking of tasks were not avoided by her, and she welcomed hard work. From her example I learned about the dignity of menial labor and the reward of going the second mile--getting as much joy and satisfaction from scrubbing a floor as from helping with an operation. Her teaching of nurses was by practical demonstration in the wards with little theory taught in the class rooms. For many years she was Colonel (Dr.) Noble's right hand both in the theater and on the wards.

"Many woman officers will remember her and salute her memory and thank God for every remembrance of her service. Her life and devoted service to Christ and the sick to whom she ministered remain with us as an inspiration and a challenge."

Brigadier Katherine Lord, a trained nurse from Virginia, USA, came as a particular asset to Colonel (Dr.) William Noble when he was setting up a new era in nurse training at the Catherine Booth Hospital, South India, in 1937 by establishing an up-to-date School of Nursing. It was "a bold and ambitious venture. Few hospitals in India had a qualified nursing school.... Few of the young women in India had a high school education or a working knowledge of English. Mohammedan families seldom allowed a daughter to become a nurse, while Brahmin and other high-caste Hindu families feared a breakdown in customs and culture if they permitted a girl to enter into such training."

Katherine Lord, "competent and qualified ... became the first nursing school superintendent.

"In the first class there were eight students. These Indian young people were all Christians, who belonged either to The Salvation Army or other missionary organizations. As the first class progressed, other young people were added to the training program.... It was a great milestone when the first R.N. certificates were presented at the Catherine Booth Hospital....

"By 1948 sixty-seven young people had been trained and registered as nurses, and twenty had further qualified as mid-wives.... All were a credit to the nursing profession." In this particular work Katherine Lord ranks as a pioneer. She was promoted to Glory in 1956, having retired from active service in 1952.

England, Canada and the USA formed the background to the preparation for missionary service of Brigadier Hilda Plummer, a volunteer for leprosy work, whose great love has been the Indian leprosy patients and their children, among whom she has served as an active and retired officer for forty-four years, her only regret being that she has not another forty-four years to give to India and to those with leprosy!

Born in Nottingham, England, to parents who had served as Salvation Army officers, Hilda Plummer had a Primitive Methodist upbringing, her father serving as a local preacher. When she was fifteen, her mother died and she went to stay with Salvationists. As a result, a week before emigrating to Canada she was enrolled as a Salvation Army soldier at Nottingham 1 Corps. It was while in Canada that she heard the testimony of a widowed English officer with four children whose husband had been promoted to Glory from the Far East. She says that it was through this testimony that the desire she had to become a missionary officer became a definite call. Not long afterwards she moved to the USA and from Troy, N.Y., entered training for Salvation Army officership and volunteered for leprosy work. A year's service as a corps officer was followed by transfer to India.

At the suggestion of Colonel (Dr.) Noble, Hilda Plummer was appointed to the Catherine Booth Hospital for two years. She had no general nursing training, but the practical experience she gained enabled her to face the challenge of opportunity when she was finally sent to the Cochin State Leprosarium, the government institution of which The Salvation Army, and Dr. Noble in particular, had the oversight.

Leprosy training at Cochin, where she was to spend many years, as well as at Chingleput, where there was a leprosy sanatorium--a Government institution but under

43

Church management--at Carville, Louisiana, which had the only leprosarium in America, enabled her to give valuable service to the patients and their families; and a first homeland furlough spent at the Mothers' Hospital, Clapton, in midwifery training, added to her usefulness.

From 1950 to 1960 Brigadier Plummer served as Superintendent in charge of the leprosarium in Bapatla, a period she regards as the happiest in her life.

"I retired in 1960", she relates. "I decided against retiring in my native England or in America. My work was not finished. I had made myself responsible for a healthy girl of leprosy parents ... so I stayed ... for her sake. I do not regret my choice.

"I am living in a nice little Indian house in an Indian village. All my neighbors are Indian; some retired officers. One mile south along the railway tracks from where I live is a village of 450 inhabitants. All except the children have leprosy. They have built little huts for themselves and lead normal family life. I help the women before the babies come and when their babies are born. Daily I thank God for giving me this little work for His Kingdom.

"You may wonder if I am happy here. The answer is: Yes, very happy. I may come home one day. I still have joy in His service more than all."

Of Gunvor Eklund, of Sweden, another nurse who has served at the Catherine Booth Hospital, Commissioner (Dr.) Harry Williams has written:

"Gunvor Eklund grew up in the village of Insjön in Dalama, Sweden. Small though it was, it had a Salvation Army corps. From it only one candidate had become a Salvation Army officer (John Hedén, 1896), and he had spent a lifetime in southern India. Every seven years, except when wars upset the program, he returned to Sweden on leave ... and on Lt. Colonel Hedén's infrequent furloughs he was invited to speak at the village school. Gunvor sat at her desk lost in wonder.... She became the second candidate, but many years were to elapse and there were many hurdles to jump before she reached Nagercoil."

Via the Mothers' Hospital, Clapton, London, Gunvor Eklund came to the Catherine Booth Hospital in South India, where "she was to tackle a wide variety of tasks ... but her abiding love has been the leprosy patients. No one can doubt their love for her. Swedish magazines began to publish articles and even collect subscriptions. The matron of her training school heard of her work and moved the trustees of a Memorial Foundation, of which she was president, to allocate funds for leprosy surgery and vocational training of young patients. Slowly the simple and relatively crude wards were transformed, and were always among the cleanest in the hospital. They were certainly the happiest, for co-operation and appreciation reach high level among crippled patients. And there was no doubt that she was their 'mother'."

"New Zealand must have the Catherine Booth Hospital engraved on her Salvation Army heart," wrote Dr. Williams (in 1970), "for she has sent so many of her sons and daughters to help. None has given more in time and energy than Brigadier Vera Williamson, the Superintendent of Nurses. Unassuming by nature, she was pitchforked into the Matron's office within her first year at the hospital.... She has ... been vigilant in watching the plans of successive Chief Medical Officers to see that due appreciation has been given to nursing needs and problems.

"Her father left the remote Shetland Islands at the age of fifteen. He travelled to Australia alone and in pique. In Australia he found a vigorous Salvation Army and joined it, but it was at Balclutha, in the South Island of New Zealand, that he found a wife from a pioneer family. Two of his daughters became officers.

"Vera says that her call was crystal clear to nursing as well as officership. She holds a diploma in nursing education and administration. She has been involved in both, serving on the State Nursing Council in its infancy. From all over the world her students write and send her gifts for the Self-Denial Fund. She has no children of her own, but hundreds of the Lord's."

Some Salvationist nurses have had to face the unqualified opposition of their families at home because of the dedication of their skills to God in The Salvation Army, and have travelled overseas without the goodwill of loved ones, often facing a certain loneliness on arrival at their appointed field of service because of being the only woman with the qualifications they hold. Typical of these was Lilian Abel, a "born" nurse, who from Manchester Star Hall entered training to become a Salvation Army officer from a non-Salvationist background, and sailed for India in 1932 in the face of strong family disapproval.

Lieutenant Abel's appointment was to the MacRobert Hospital, Dhariwal, North-Eastern India. Built in 1926 on land leased from the British India Woolen Mills, and named after the Director of the time, the hospital was to provide a medical service for the employees of the mill in return for the lease, as well as serving the surrounding district. Dr. Samuel Burfoot was the M.O. at the time, and Nurse Abel the only member of the staff holding S.R.N. and S.C.M. qualifications. This remained the case until the arrival, four years later, of Major Margaret Mouat, a devoted Scottish officer. Lilian Abel afterwards served at the Thomas Emery Hospital, Moradabad, as Matron from 1939 to 1949, holding rank as Lt. Colonel in the Indian Medical Service in war years, and being awarded the high honor, Royal Red Cross (1st Class): Margaret Mouat was to complete 23½ years in Dhariwal, seeing the hospital grow in capacity from 40 beds to 100 and become a Nurse's Training School under Dr. Harry Williams.

By 1946 Lilian Abel's family had become reconciled to the fact that she was doing the work to which she had felt called by God. Today, as a retired Salvation Army Lt. Colonel, Lilian Abel writes: "I have no regrets. There have been many times of doubting, times of disappointment, but these have been greatly outweighed by the joy of service and the knowledge that God was, as I believe, using me--in even a small way--to bring blessing and help to others. There was always a deep sense of peace in the assurance that His grace and strength were-- and still are--sufficient for every experience of daily living."

Africa, as well as India, has had its quota of valiant nurses, and the story of Brigadier Mary Styles (Mary of

Vendaland) links this intrepid officer, awarded The Salvation Army's highest honor--the Order of the Founder-- in 1965, with a warrior-nurse of earlier times, Major Agatha Battersby, of New Zealand, who introduced Mary Styles to the people and life she was to make peculiarly her own in the northern wilds of South Africa.

"Bred in the clean white town of Queenstown, in the Cape," Mary Styles had first made a dedication to God's service in an Anglican Church in Queenstown, when "listening to an elderly and revered sister speaking about the differing ways in which God called people to His service, and about unexpected places to which they were called." To her own surprise, Mary found herself declaring, "And He's called me to be a Salvation Army officer." At the time she knew little about "the Army," except for its open-air meetings, but eventually she became a Salvationist and an officer.

When, as a Lieutenant, she was told that she was to be sent to Vendaland she hardly knew where the place was, its location "tucked away in the extreme northern mountains and plains of South Africa, against the borders of Rhodesia and Portuguese East Africa." Here The Salvation Army had a settlement, named after William Eadie, one of its early leaders. The District Officer, Adjutant Agatha Battersby, was in charge and Adjutant Mashau, a kindly African, provided male support. The newly-appointed Lieutenant was expected to assist with all that needed to be done, from the cleaning of undergrowth and the making of bricks to assistance with the midwifery and the teaching of children to read. Adjutant Battersby was an untiring worker and Mary watched and listened; and learned, as she worked, to cope with clinics, sickness, childbirth and accidents. The main problem at the settlement, part of which was used by the two women as living quarters, was lack of room, in a place that served also as a clinic, hospital, hall, classroom and headquarters!

"Successful as a bricklayer, Battersby decided they must have a water tank. Mary learned how to use a spade and the tank was made--by digging a hole as large as a room, facing it with bricks and concrete, and then covering the top with zinc sheets which could be removed during rains."

Besides coping herself with the kind of emergency that arose from a crocodile bite, a mishandled birth, a dental crisis and other demands, on many occasions Mary, with the other two officers as companions, "would complete a circuit of the district's corps, tramping over the mountains and through the bush--wading rivers and swamps.... Sometimes at night, the party would camp in some remote spot, where Mashau would build a huge fire to scare away unwanted companions." Wildlife abounded in the area!

For eight years Mary lived this wilderness life, before being given opportunity officially to train at Durban for the nursing job to which she had so long been apprenticed. Perhaps it was for this very reason that, having after much toil and application qualified as a nurse and midwife and given service at the Army's hospitals at Cape Town, she began to feel some revulsion at the idea of returning to Vendaland. When orders finally came to do so, she agreed to go "for a couple of weeks" but soon found herself deeply involved with the Ba Venda (the Venda people) some of whom, remembering her from former days, hailed her return with excited delight, crying, "The Captain's back! The Captain's back!" From that moment the Ba Venda became her people. It was for her service to them that General Frederick Coutts in 1965 admitted her to the Order of the Founder, the citation declaring: "Brigadier Mary Styles: has for more than twenty years, from the South Africa Territory's most remote medical station, given devoted care to the Ba Venda."

The William Eadie Settlement became a busy complex of square concrete buildings including the divisional headquarters office, a corps, a hospital clinic and officers' quarters, and her biographer wrote: "The ambulance Brigadier Mary Styles, O.F., drives is equipped with a gleaming modern stretcher trolley. But when she is descending the giddy crags of the Zoutzpansberg and tramping the long dusty leagues under the burning Venda skies," she still finds "the sack with a couple of poles thrust through is the most practical way to carry a bulky patient."

If the people learned to call Mary Styles "Grandmother", or "Mother Styles", "the title has none of the disparagement it sometimes carries for Europeans: it is the most dignified title an African woman can receive."

In a farewell tribute to her, when in 1970 Brigadier Mary Styles took leave of those with whom she had worked for so long, the Commissioner General for the Venda and Tsonga ethnic groups wrote:

"In the darkest moments of the lives of many Venda, Brigadier Styles was there to save, to nurse and to serve. Through this work she has built for herself a lasting monument in the hearts of the Venda. I have been struck by the way they, without exception, talk about 'Mother Styles'. To them she was a mother in the real sense of the word.... I am convinced that the name 'Mother Styles' will always be remembered in the greatest gratitude by the Venda."

In 1950 Ghana was on the verge of independence, the first of the new nations of Africa to emerge from colonial rule. Economically independent, through the boom in cocoa and mahogany, and free of white settlers and color problems, it was still bound by superstition and ignorance in many aspects of life, and burdened by disease. From the verge of the Sahara in the north came periodic outbreaks of meningitis brought south by the Hausa cattle dealers. In the forest was bred the tsetse fly with its load of malaria, tropical ulcers and intestinal diseases that had earned the west coast of Africa its non-welcoming title of "White Man's Grave."

Begoro, on an escarpment ninety miles inland from Accra, was a large native town surrounded by cocoa farms and forests rich in mahogany. There The Salvation Army had a large corps, under Captain Benjamin Amu, and a primary school of eight classes under an Australian Lieutenant, Jessie Jenks. It was not The Salvation Army's intention to station a young woman officer alone in a place miles from other Europeans. A married couple, due to arrive at the same time as the Lieutenant, had been unable to come. After a year as the only overseas officer, the Lieutenant received the wonderful news that the first Salvation Army clinic in Ghana was to be opened at Begoro and a nurse was on her way. What excitement in the corps! What rejoicing in the whole town!

On the great day, all the corps, school children and hangers-on marched out to wait for the Divisional

Commander's car a mile or so outside the town. From the car emerged a pocket-sized nurse: Captain Agnes Cage. She had served for a time in China and in Korea, but had been flown home for medical treatment. By the time she was ready for duty the door had closed for her return to the Far East. But she willingly agreed to serve in Africa. Triple qualified and experienced, she packed tremendous energy in her small frame. She possessed both a friendly nature and a fierce temper that was to accomplish a great deal when it flared out at shopkeepers selling dangerous drugs bought from pedlars! Because of her almost pure gold hair she was regarded as "ancient," a source of amusement to the Lieutenant, since the Captain at the time was only thirty or so, but a factor earning her respect from the Africans. This was heightened by the fact that the Chief named her after his grandmother, raising her to high standing in the community.

Now, as she stepped from the car smiling at the crowd, she was ushered to the head of the procession and marched for two or three miles in the tropical midday sun, through the town. The Chief came out on to his dais under the sacred tree in the town's center. The Presbyterians rang the two big bells in their church tower to show their participation in the general rejoicing. The "mammy doctor" had come.

There were no materials to start with, save the supplies she had brought with her. The chief loaned a building until the clinic was erected. With a seventeen-year-old girl to translate, the Captain-nurse examined and treated the women and children who came in droves. For a long time no men came. But one day she was called to a house to see a man with pneumonia. In a few days he was up and about again, after being close to death. From then on the "mammy doctor" had men as well as women and children on her list.

The maternity cases were the most worrying. The women didn't send for her unless something was wrong. Almost all the summons were night calls, and both officers would be awake as soon as any light was to be seen moving in the village, and be dressed by the time a voice called, "*Agoo!*" outside. That is, the English girl would be dressed, and the "Aussie" Lieutenant pulled mosquito boots over her pyjama-legs and a dress over her pyjama jacket and insisted that the costume was perfectly in order since it looked all right! Rather green and raw, she went along at night in order to ask the necessary questions and throw out interfering grandmothers! Nothing terrified her more than being given a slimy, choking baby to dangle by the heels, while the nurse coped with the mother, and her fear that she might drop the infant on his head was often shared by the grandmother, who objected to this type of draining and was waiting to carry the naked babe out in the cold night to show it to the father.

One day, the "mammy doctor" came to the school, holding a telegram. It was signed "Leprosy Doctor" and asked her to assemble leprosy sufferers on a given date. "Are there any here in the town, or outside?" she asked. The two women officers went off to their "very present help," Captain Amu. "Yes, there are some in the town and in the farms."

"But how do I assemble them? I'm not sure I'd recognize one if I saw one."

"Leave it to me, Captain. I'll ask the Chief to beat the talking drum, and everyone will know."

So once more the problem was left in Captain Amu's capable hands. The women officers heard the drum beating. Its message, unintelligible to them, was obeyed; and when the Government doctor arrived the patients were there. Was "Sister" willing to hold a leprosy clinic and issue DADPS and check reactions? "Sister" expressed herself willing but ignorant. So for several hours the sweating pair examined patients together, the doctor explained symptoms and side-effects and the sister listened and learned. From then on the sufferers came regularly for their treatment.

Another day it was the local policeman who arrived. A man had cut his throat. Would sister come and write out a medical report?

"Is he dead?"

"No, but soon to die." was the reply in the West Coast pidgin. Salvation Army Captains do not use bad language to police constables. Let us say a kind of snarl slipped out as "mammy doctor" snatched up bandages and raced to the police post. The man was still alive when she had finished her first aid. She sent for a local truck driver. He was unenthusiastic about taking the man twenty-five miles to hospital: he would surely die and haunt the lorry. Then the Captain, who had been gently dripping milk into the man's mouth, paused in her labor of love and drew herself up to her full "five feet nothing" and blazed. In a little while, a terrified policeman was instructing the cringing driver to get his patient to the hospital with every care and diligence. Hangers-around were fading into the background with all speed, while the Captain enlarged on the topic of the report she would be sending if....

A few weeks later the man returned with his throat neatly healed, and the "mammy doctor" was greeted with even more veneration than before. The children loved her. They could not understand, of course, what she said to the mothers who tried to cure baby's cold by stuffing red pepper in its ears and nostrils.

On Saturday mornings the two women officers wandered through the village shops and market, buying a tin of fish here and some bananas there, but in actual fact keeping an eye open to see what medicines were on sale. Pilfering from Government hospitals was not uncommon and "M and B 693" was regarded as a cure-all. After a fight to save the Chief's wife, who had taken an overdose in blissful ignorance, the "mammy doctor" was on the lookout for the source. This led to the Saturday rambles through the shops, the two usually escorted by a group of small children. One woman rebuked a little tot for clinging to the Captain's white skirt with grubby hands. Proudly the tot replied, "When I go to the clinic, she sits me on her knee."

The story is one without an end, for it is a recurring one in different places, with different people still needing a "mammy doctor" to love, bully and cajole them.

Emilia van Hoogstraten was already a fully-trained nursing sister when, from the Netherlands, she entered The Salvation Army's International Training College in London in 1932. Possessed of a burning spirit of evangelism, she found her first appointment--to the training college staff, for service in the health lodge--severely chafing to her ardent spirit with its desire to be "out among the people" and working for the poorest and most needy. She discovered means of fulfilling her longing, however, in the surrounding Camberwell district and would be off alone, whenever her duties permitted, to seek out and help the poor and churchless of the area.

Returning to her native Netherlands, she was given an appointment nearer to her heart, though several times, while engaged in midnight work, her life was in peril. Danger was to be a recurring factor in Emilia's service as an officer-nurse. She was stationed in her own country when, in 1940, the German military breakthrough occurred and the Dutch training college was quickly turned into a first aid post. For a period she nursed the wounded day and night, a strong physique serving her well in the crisis. Later she was appointed to Belgium and, hearing from returning missionary officers of the great needs of the Congo, volunteered for that field.

Though not brought up as a Salvationist, Emilia van Hoogstraten breathes naturally, what is known in the Movement as "the Army spirit." In a personal letter, written from Equatorial Africa following a time of political upheaval and heavy fighting in the early 1960s, she described something of her experiences: "You know that during the September war, I was in Katanga. There was very much to do for the wounded. I tried to do what I could for them, spiritually and materially. There was very great suffering in the four hospitals (Elisabethville)...." Some of the patients she tended had encountered unspeakable horrors.

A report to International Headquarters said: "Elisabethville has been cut off from the rest of the territory for months but Brigadier E. van Hoogstraten has worked with great devotion among her people."

Having to cross the border to Ndola (then in Northern Rhodesia) for supplies just before Christmas, Brigadier van Hoogstraten found herself unable to get back to Katanga, as fighting had broken out in the area. "I could not go back," she wrote, "I could only help the thousands of refugees who came through." The modest statement covered a period of strenuous and often heart-breaking activity.

On her return to Elisabethville, she was to write: "The Salvation Army is the first mission to be back in town and the Katanga soldiers at the border cheered me. 'The Salvation Army is back! Good! Good!' they called out." Her reception by her own African comrades was deeply moving. Going immediately to the largest of the corps, she was joyfully reunited with her friends. "You should have seen them," she wrote. "There was dancing and rejoicing. I felt like a mother coming home to her children." She never failed to pay tribute to the courage of her African comrades, and her account of the African officer who made his way through the firing in the streets to make contact with her would bring tears to her eyes as she recalled the incident.

Soon after this, she found herself distributing relief and acting as padre and goodwill officer, as well as divisional officer. But every added responsibility was joyfully borne for the sake of the people she was serving. "I thank the Lord every day for placing me here," was her testimony. To friends in Europe her only request was for a continuance of prayer on her behalf. "It is so strengthening to know that you, with many others, are praying for me," she told them. "There is nothing like prayer: it is the strongest weapon in our warfare." She was referring, of course, to the spiritual battle the Salvationist constantly wages.

When the official time came for her retirement, Emilia van Hoogstraten was--as might be imagined--reluctant to leave the African comrades with whom she had so closely identified herself, but a period of residence in Marseilles, where she was able to develop a ministry of her own to African seaman in this cosmopolitan port, helped her to feel she was still serving her beloved Africa, albeit from across the sea. A largely unsung heroine, Emilia is typical of many nurses whose service has been unstintingly given in the missionary field, above and beyond the call of duty.

AIDS MINISTRY IN ZAMBIA

From: "The War Cry"

Published by
The Salvation Army
National Headquarters
Verona, N.J., USA (April 1, 1989)

Sara was the mother of four children. To support her family she engaged in sexual relations with truck drivers who passed her house in Zambia.

When she became ill she entered The Salvation Army's Chikankata Hospital. Lab tests revealed that she was HIV+. She was a victim of AIDS.

AIDS patients at other hospitals in Zambia are informed of the diagnosis, then sent home. They are forced to bear a virtual death sentence alone. But this did not happen to Sara. At Chikankata, Christian professionals minister to patients, their families and their villages. As they do, they seek opportunities to help prevent the spread of the deadly disease.

The AIDS care and prevention team from Chikankata visited Sara regularly in her home. They came to see whether her condition had worsened and to help her family care for her.

Team members were concerned for more than Sara's physical needs, though. They listened as she expressed feelings of guilt because of her lifestyle and the problems it had caused her children. They heard her when she said she was afraid to die.

Through every stage of her illness, the team continued their visits. Just before her death the team social worker helped her express her guilt and fear to God and experience forgiveness. After that, she found the peace she needed to accept her death.

Sara's story has been repeated more than 230 times in the villages surrounding Chikankata, for that is the number of patients visited by the AIDS team through last September. In each instance, team members have demonstrated practical compassion for everyone whose lives they touch.

The support they give family members does not end when a patient dies. For example, team members usually attend funerals as a reminder of their continuing commitment to the community.

When they attended the funeral of a former patient named Lackson, his mother said that their presence was proof that he had been greatly loved.

At the request of the family, the team read Scripture and prayed--and made the customary contribution of money. By the time the team left, family members had abandoned their traditional wailing and said they had seen God that day.

The AIDS care unit at Chikankata is a recent development. It was not until 1986 that staff members at Chikankata, as in the rest of Zambia, noted an increasing number of patients with the AIDS virus.

Only in the past few years has AIDS been identified as a major health problem in Africa. But it is a problem that is growing rapidly. At least one million Africans will die of AIDS in the next ten years. According to the Panos Institute, an international information agency, most of them will be from central Africa.

Zambia is part of that region, the so-called AIDS belt. In one year about 6,000 babies were born to Zambian mothers with the AIDS virus! Of those babies, 50% died in their first year.

While AIDS is linked with homosexuality and drug use in the U.S., the entire African population is acutely susceptible to the disease. According to Alison Rader, project manager for the team, "You can't talk in terms of risk groups. There's no such thing. The virus pool is large enough that *any* sexually active person is at risk."

In March 1987 a social agency proposed that an AIDS hospice care facility be added to the Salvation Army Hospital at Chikankata. But Captain (Dr.) Ian Campbell, chief medical officer at the hospital, found the plan inappropriate for Zambia. No facility would have been large enough for the expected increase in victims of AIDS.

Dr. Campbell, the driving force behind the AIDS care unit, also understood that the greatest resource of Zambia is the extended family. He knew that any successful AIDS prevention program would have to build on the strengths of the family.

In addition, staff members also realized that rural Zambians prefer to die at home with their families caring for them.

The challenge facing the staff of Chikankata was to make use of the family network before a whole generation of young adults is lost. The solution they devised is an innovative program using hospital skills and facilities but whose main component is a home-based care and prevention team.

As they did for Sara, the team visits AIDS patients in their villages regularly. During these visits, always at the patient's request, team members determine patient and family needs. They also conduct education sessions with the patient, the family and, where possible, the wider community.

Patient care is one of the important reasons for the visits. But the ultimate goal, crucial to the future of Zambia, is the prevention of AIDS. The focus of the team's efforts is to assist family members as they take responsibility for their actions and change behavior where necessary.

It is too soon to measure the effectiveness of the AIDS team. However, Alison Rader speaks of the work as being "terribly encouraging. Our first conversations have been received far more positively than we ever expected. We're going to communities and talking to them and they are saying, 'Yes, we have to do something.'" Recently, through the team's influence a local chief changed a longstanding tradition of ritual cleansing by sexual intercourse to safer methods.

Like other Zambians, the chief has discovered that he can rely on the judgment of Chikankata staff members. Dr. Clement Chela, a Zambian, asked a patient for permission to conduct blood tests. The man replied, "Doctor, my body and my spirit are in your hands, so do what you need to do to help me." The integrity and character of the Christians who minister with the AIDS care unit justifies such faith--and may be the key to the future of Zambia itself.

GENERAL BOOTH AS FAITH HEALER

By Thomas F. G. Coates

From "The Prophet of the Poor"

Published by
Hodder and Stoughton
London (1905)

It is the doctrine of General Booth and The Salvation Army that the sick can be healed as the direct result of faith and prayer. His teaching on the subject, briefly summarized, is that "by faith-healing, or Divine healing, is to be understood the recovery of persons afflicted with serious diseases, by the power of God, in answer to faith and prayer, without the use of ordinary means, such as doctors, medicines, and the like." It is so set out in the orders and regulations for field officers written by the General, and consequently it is an accepted article of belief on the part of each field officer.

The question is of great importance, and always has been, and still is, a very controversial one. General Booth found that within the Army views were put forward with regard to it "which are contrary to our orders and regulations and opposed to the teaching of Scripture, and which, if received among us, would be calculated to create controversy, and thereby interfere with the peace, power, and progress of the Army."

For this reason General Booth came to the conclusion that the matter required to be dealt with in a special manner, and he consequently issued a memorandum on the subject for the use of officers of the Army. Numerous instances of faith-healing have, he declares, occurred within his experience, and he claims that St. James provides biblical teaching in favor of this method of healing. He finds proof of it in the passage, James 5:14, 15: "Is any sick among you? Let him call for the elders of the Church; and let them pray over him, anointing him with oil in the name of the Lord: and the prayer of faith shall save the sick, and the Lord shall raise him up; and if he have committed sins they shall be forgiven him." The healing of the sick directly by the power of God has from the beginning, he tells his officers, been associated with the office of prophets, priests, teachers, apostles, and, indeed, of all those, known by whatever name, who have been the agents of God on the earth.

"From the beginning there can be no question that God has also been pleased to heal sickness and disease by the use of appropriate means. He has, it is true, in some instances chosen to preserve health without food; but, as a rule, if men want to keep health they must use suitable means. Just so with the restoration of health when it is lost."

That there is direct answer to believing prayer is, therefore, one of the articles of faith of The Salvation Army, and the columns of *The War Cry* have contained reports of such cases which lead General Booth to the conclusion that there cannot be a corps of The Salvation Army, at home or abroad, in which signs and wonders have not been wrought to support this theory of faith-healing.

"Have we not seen," he says, "men and women and little children raised up from the borders of the grave, and restored to health and vigor, in answer to the prayer of faith? Have we not seen cures effected in a moment when every human means has been tried, but tried to fail? When kindred and friends have been in absolute despair, and when the sufferers themselves had concluded that there was no healing of them in this life, has not God appeared to them, have they not been raised up, to go in and out among us again praising Him, and are not some of them with us today, and have not some of them since passed away, glorifying the prayer-answering God on triumphant dying beds?"

Obviously if the expression of belief in faith-healing were left to the definitions thus given it would be easy to misrepresent the attitude of The Salvation Army in this regard. General Booth found that was the case, and he supplemented the definitions by a full expression of opinion on "views which have been set forth on the subject of faith-healing that are false, misleading, and ruinous. Against their acceptance I want to caution the officers-- not only because they are untrue, but because I know them to be dangerous and productive of evil to those who embrace them, and because I cannot therefore permit them to be taught among us, either in our publications, in our meetings, or to our people in any other form, by either officers, soldiers, or any one else."

General Booth therefore directed his officers thus: "It must not be taught in The Salvation Army that sickness is necessarily an evidence of the presence of sin in the persons afflicted.

"It must not be taught among us that all sickness in His people is contrary to the will of God. If this doctrine were true, then the precious grace of resignation has no place in the chambers of human suffering, and the afflicted and dying saints have all been mistaken in saying and thinking, 'This is God's Way. His will be done.' Such a teaching strikes at the very root of all real union with God, and almost makes the prayer of the Lord Jesus Himself to be wrong, when, in His acute physical as well as mental anguish, He cried out in the garden, 'Oh, My Father, if it be possible, let this cup pass from Me: nevertheless, not as I will, but as Thou wilt.'

"It must not be taught that Jesus Christ has, by His loving sacrifice, redeemed the body as He has redeemed the soul. Or, in other words, that He has procured health for the body in this life in the same sense that He procured salvation for the soul.

"It must not be taught that when disease is not healed in answer to prayer, or when death follows as the result of sickness, it is the result of the unbelief of the sufferer.

"It must not be taught among us that those who exercise faith in God for healing are cured when there is evidence that they are not.

"It must not be taught among us that it is contrary to the will of God that means should be used for the recovery of the sick."

Regarding the last-mentioned point much controversy has raged, and General Booth has done well to leave no shadow of doubt as to his conviction on this point and what the Army officers are instructed to teach. While it is claimed that the Almighty could accomplish everything without means, the assertion is emphatic that the use of means has not been dispensed with.

"It is no part of the work of Salvationists," says the General, "to take up cudgels for or against any particular species of physic or any particular school of physicians. No doubt many members of each of the medical schools are highly capable, devoted, and laborious toilers, as far as they have light, for the highest welfare of humanity, even if others, belonging to the self-seeking class, are reckless of the welfare of their fellows so long as they can profit by them.

"But that is not the question. Our discussion is not as to whether it is right or wrong to have recourse to physicians or to use drugs, but whether it is right to employ any means at all for the healing of bodily sicknesses. And the answer I make to that question is, that the neglect or non-use of such means as are within our power, and which, according to the knowledge we have, seem likely to alleviate suffering in sickness, or to help recovery from it, or to prolong life, is a very serious mistake--a mistake that is contrary to the teaching of Scripture, of Providence, of Common Sense, of Humanity, and of True Religion. And, more than this, it is a mistake which must, I am satisfied, result in disastrous consequences to those who make it."

General Booth is too practical in all his ways to ignore the use of the means provided to produce any good work. He is an active enemy of the Christian fatalist and the sleeper on faith. He believes that those are most helped who show their desire to do what in them lies to deserve help. Man, he points out, must eat, and wash, and dress, and sleep to live. Continuing his argument on the use of means to cure infirmities, he says: "Every now and then small cliques of people have risen up who have boasted that God would keep them in being, and in well-being, without the use of food. But they have not endured for any great length of time. Some one was telling me the other day of a sect of people who came into existence in a certain place who boasted that they were to exist forever. They call themselves Angelites, the peculiarity of their creed and practice being that they frequently soaked their feet in hot mustard and water and abstained from food! On asking what became of them, we were not surprised to hear that they soon died out! 'If a man will not work, neither shall he eat,' the apostle says; and if he does not eat we know that he will not live.

"Why, then," asks General Booth, "should the healing of the body be an exception to this all but universal law? Why should not natural means be as necessary, as religious, as really in harmony with the Divine plan for the recovery of health as for its preservation? The natural instincts of the race approve the propriety and necessity for the employment of means for the alleviation and removal of human suffering, from whatever source it may spring. Everywhere there is a spirit in man which says, 'Do what in you lies to heal sickness, to relieve pain, and conserve life.' When there is a shipwreck and the sailors, half drowned, are landed by the lifeboat on the shore; when there is a fire, and half dead with scalds, or burns, or suffocation, the women and the children are dragged out of the fire-escape; when there is a battle, and the soldiers are found with faces and limbs torn and shattered by shot and shell, what do men or women, foes or friends, suggest? Would humanity, common sense, or Christianity at such times say, 'Let us do nothing but lay them down, and pray and believe, and wait on God for the relief or cure of all these agonies?' No, everyone knows that the reply of all, whether strangers or friends would be: 'Use the means-- such means as you have at hand. Have faith in God while you use them, but use the means most likely to help the sufferers, and do so at once.'"

The General also argues that the threatenings of the Bible are against those who neglect the use of means, that the faith enjoined by the Bible is the faith which works by means, and that the miracles of the Bible, rather than being opposed in their lessons to the employment of means, strongly favor their use. In the injunction to the sick even to call in the elders and be by them anointed with oil, he points out the very practical means there called to the assistance of faith, inasmuch as oil was one of the most useful and popular remedies known in the Eastern world, and that it is still employed in the treatment of disease to an enormous extent, both internally and externally, the anointing which the Apostle urged being no mere symbol but application of a simple and universally approved remedy. General Booth's "faith-healing" is a simple and practical theory of first causes-- that whether the sick man is healed through the agency of direct Divine interposition or through the influence of medicine, or of water, or food, or oil, God is behind all these influences and means.

III. Lust

Introducing this subject, the Founder writes, "The third river to which I refer derives its force and energy, if not its very existence, from vicious indulgences. It may be described as The Unlawful Gratification of the Physical Appetites.

"In hearts and homes, where happiness might reign, where abundance might flourish, and where love might abound, you have miseries resembling the agonies of Hell itself, miseries brought about by the thoughtless, selfish, and wicked conduct of those who suffer them. One half of the miseries of the world flow from this source."

Is there a solution? Booth declares, "Salvation will deliver him from its bondage, and from the various forms of evil associated with his particular besetment."

Lust (The Unlawful Gratification of the Physical Appetites)
(from *Darkest England*)

The difficulty of dealing with drunkards and harlots is almost insurmountable. Were it not that I utterly repudiate as a fundamental denial of the essential principle of the Christian religion the popular pseudo-scientific doctrine that any man or woman is past saving by the grace of God and the power of the Holy Spirit, I would sometimes be disposed to despair when contemplating these victims of the Devil.

... Thousands upon thousands of these poor wretches are ... not so much born into this world as damned into it. The bastard of a harlot, born in a brothel, suckled on gin, and familiar from earliest infancy with all the bestialities of debauch, violated before she is twelve, and driven out into the streets by her mother a year or two later, what chance is there for such a girl in this world--to say nothing about the next? (pages 54-55)

With boys it is almost as bad. There are thousands who were begotten when both parents were besotted with drink, whose mothers saturated themselves with alcohol every day of their pregnancy, who may be said to have sucked in a taste for strong drink with their mothers' milk. (page 55)

The drink difficulty lies at the root of everything. Nine-tenths of our poverty, squalor, vice, and crime spring from this poisonous tap-root. Many of our social evils ... would dwindle away and die if they were not constantly watered with strong drink. (page 55)

Vice offers to every good-looking girl during the first bloom of her youth and beauty more money than she can earn by labor in any field of industry open to her sex. The penalty exacted afterwards is disease, degradation and death.... The profession of a prostitute is the only career in which the maximum income is paid to the newest apprentice.... (page 59)

THE ARMY'S SOCIAL REVOLUTION IN JAPAN

By Henry Bullard

From "The Staff Review"

Published by
The Salvation Army
International Headquarters
London (October 1926)

The story is a quarter of a century old, but it is worth repeating as that of perhaps the greatest social triumph of the Army in any land. Added interest and perhaps increased significance are given to the achievement in view of its having taken place in Japan, in the earliest days of our work there, when our corps did not number a dozen and the officers totalled less than two score. The nation was then in the middle of its remarkable evolution from medievalism, isolation, and obscurity, and was anxious, by attention to internal national conditions, as well as international relationships, to secure the confidence, respect, and goodwill of the great nations outside.

With these aspirations there had also grown up a very strong sentiment in opposition to the system of Government-controlled vice that had existed for centuries-- a system which had become abhorrent and which, it was considered, sullied the fair fame of the Empire. These tendencies were undoubtedly important factors and contributed in no small measure to the success of our campaign against the social evil.

At the time all immoral houses were gathered together in certain districts, usually on the outskirts of a city or town. The more important of the Licensed Quarters were surrounded by a high fence, with but one main entrance. In Tokyo with its population of two and a half million, there were five of these districts, the chief being the Yoshawara. All the houses in these districts were licensed by the Government for immoral purposes. Every female inmate was similarly licensed, and a register of them was kept by the police of the district. *In the Yoshawara alone there were over 5,000 licensed inmates,* with approximately the same number of male attendants. When once a young woman had been licensed and entered upon this life of shame, it was practically impossible for her to abandon it, whatever might be her disinclination to continue it or physical disability. Often they were under-fed and cruelly treated. Sometimes the life became so hateful to them that they would try to escape but it invariably resulted in their being arrested by the police, punished for running away, and then returned to the house from which they had escaped and forced to continue this life.

The girls were obtained by brothel-keepers making a loan to the parents or guardians. The girls, not knowing in many cases what it entailed, contracted to remain and live a life of shame until the loan was repaid. A famine, earthquake, epidemic, or any other national disaster which produced financial stringency and poverty, was a harvest season for the brothel-keepers. The loans made to the parents or guardians of the girls were supposed to be repaid by the income produced from the shame of their daughters, but the accounts of the girls were kept by the brothel-keepers, who were almost without exception avaricious, brutal, and unscrupulous. The consequence was that the debt, instead of decreasing, gradually increased. The supposed income was never equal even to the cost of their maintenance. The friends were seldom, if ever, in a position to repay the accumulated debt for maintenance added to the original loan, and therefore these young women became literal slaves, bound by law to this life of sin, until they became physically useless or were released by death.

Thus the fairest maidenhood of the land was annually sacrificed on the altar of vice. They were generally induced to barter their purity from a false notion of their duty to assist their distressed family, and in this respect they were actuated by high motives. Such action had always been looked upon as a virtue, and the victim did not lose the love and respect of her friends because of what was regarded as a meritorious act of self-sacrifice.

On my appointment to the command of the Army's work in Japan, in 1900, I was anxious to extend not only its spiritual but its social activities, and in view of the terrible conditions I have described, it appeared expedient that Rescue Work such as had been so successful in other lands should be established. But we were faced by apparently insuperable difficulties. Neither we nor the girls' friends could pay the enormous sums demanded for the release of many of these girls, and it was an indictable offence to take them away from the control of their masters until their accumulated debts had been paid. It was known, too, that the brothel-keepers and their satellites--the most reckless and depraved characters of the nation--would resort to any degree of violence to prevent attempts to release their victims and thus deprive themselves of their legal financial rights.

We decided to make the attempt, though it certainly was considered by all whom we consulted to be a foolish and hopeless venture.

The first thing was to establish an institution into which we could invite girls who desired our help, and Lt. Commissioner and Mrs. Yamamuro, with heroic spirit of self-sacrifice, offered to take the oversight of such a home.

The next consideration was how to make our plans known among the girls whom we desired to help. We decided to issue a special Rescue Number of our Japanese *War Cry*, devoted to showing the evils of such a life of sin, the power of God to save from it, and our willingness to help and protect any girl who would come to us. It was expedient that our people should go individually to distribute *The War Cry* in the immoral quarters. We therefore arranged to make an organized attack on these haunts of vice. Our officers at a number of corps were instructed how to proceed.

In Tokyo the officers and soldiers assembled at the hall in Kanda, an important district of the city, and then marched with flag flying, drum beating, and with Army songs, through the main entrance to the notorious Yoshawara Licensed Quarter. Our entrance caused considerable excitement, and a great concourse of visitors to these houses and male attendants crowded around. Our small band halted at various street corners, stated the object of our visit and distributed the special Rescue *War Cry* among the girls who flocked outside the houses to see what was happening. An invitation was given to these to forsake their life of sin and come to our Rescue Home. As soon as our aim was understood, an uproar began. We were violently attacked by the men. They smashed our drum, tore our flag to shreds, and beat and wounded all members of our little band, who with difficulty escaped, cut and bruised, and made their way back to the hall from which we had started.

This might have seemed an utter defeat, but it was what we had anticipated. It obtained the publicity we required for our purpose, though at a cost of considerable suffering.

The next morning the principle newspapers were full of details of our attack on the Licensed Quarters, giving lengthy extracts from our Rescue *War Cry* and advertising the fact that we had established a Rescue Home. Editors and reporters from all the leading papers came to interview me, and police officials came to ask our object and intentions. All wanted to know *why* we did it. We explained our object, but they all argued that, human nature being what it was, and the social evil existing as it did, it was necessary that it should be controlled in the existing manner. We answered that we were not immediately concerned about the system, but that our point was that any girl who wished to abandon her life of sin ought to have opportunity to do so.

Our reasoning appealed both to the police and the newspaper men, and our obvious sincerity, purity of motive, and courage gained their support. The Government officers and police were especially sympathetic throughout the whole agitation. They were with us in our aims and rendered constant and invaluable aid. They showed that they were as anxious as we were for the removal of a great and flagrant national social evil. The newspapers, with scarcely an exception, took sides with us, emphasized the evils of the system, and urged that the law should be changed so that it might be possible for any woman or girl in the Licensed Quarters to return to the paths of virtue. This started an agitation that stirred the nation to an extent that it had never previously been stirred on any social subject. For many days the papers devoted most of their space to this question.

We received a great many letters from girls asking for assistance in gaining their liberty. The keepers, however, were on their guard, but we took what steps were necessary. What rejoicing there was when a jinricksha brought the first released girl to our home! In view of subsequent happenings, it was really an historic event. Soon other girls followed, and we had one home full. We were naturally full of fear as to what action would be taken by the authorities, and we were in constant anxiety from fear of an attack by the brothel-keepers and their satellites.

We toured through the country, conducting crowded meetings, in which we explained what we were doing and

71

quickened interest in the Social Campaign. This tour was full of exciting and interesting incidents. The agitation increased daily, and all our movements and actions were given the fullest publicity. The police made constant inquiries at the home, but took no action to remove any of the girls from our care. The hand of God was on the brothel-keepers, so that they never attacked one home, as they might have been expected to do.

Some of the girls who saw the newspaper accounts of our campaign appealed imploringly to the editors for help, with the result that several editors, with members of their staffs, forcibly secured the release of a number of girls. The conditions in the Licensed Quarters became the chief topic of public interest and of conversation. The Japanese newspapers had never previously issued special editions, but the excitement was so great, that the Tokyo papers began the issue of two and even three editions daily.

Stirring incidents were connected with every girl we rescued, and some of our attempts were frustrated. On one occasion Lt. Commissioners Duce and Yamamuro and a number of other officers went to secure the release of a girl who had appealed to us, but they were attacked and so badly cut and bruised, that they bear the marks in their bodies to this day. On another occasion I went to the Yoshawara with a party of comrades in response to the piteous appeal of a sick inmate. Over fifty policemen accompanied us, but when we entered the Licensed Quarters, we were immediately surrounded by several hundred rowdies armed with sticks and other weapons. Accompanied by the police, we went into an office to demand from the chief of the brothel-keepers the release of this particular girl. A menacing crowd of several thousand men gathered outside and, though the police received reinforcements, they were powerless to deal with the mob, and ultimately forced us to leave by an unused exit to escape the violence of the crowds.

As a consequence of our campaign and the publicity given in the Press, the number of visitors to these haunts of vice began to decrease so rapidly, that the keepers placed pickets at the entrance of the Licensed Quarters to examine and prevent any one entering who was either a Salvationist or a member of the staff of a newspaper. A number of visitors who were supposed by the pickets to be

pressman, were well beaten and prevented from entering!
Some licensed houses had to be closed because of the loss
of inmates and the decrease in the number of visitors.
This so maddened the keepers, that they came out and
attacked the offices of two of the leading newspapers,
seriously injured members of the staff, and did a great
deal of damage to the property and machinery.

The police, anxious to protect us, placed constables
outside the quarters of myself and the Chief Secretary.
For several months we lived in constant anticipation of
attacks by mobs or individuals. For nearly a year our
houses were thus guarded by special police, and for a time
we were personally shadowed by police wherever we went.
In view of the reckless character of those engaged in this
terrible traffic, it was plain evidence of God's care that
there was no loss of life.

While all of this was taking place in Tokyo, a number
of girls appealed to us from the Provinces, and hundreds
of distressed parents sought our help. The following is a
translation of a sample of the letters received:

Kobe,
August 14, 1900

DEAR OFFICERS OF THE SALVATION ARMY,

    I am a poor helpless girl forced to take up a
life of sin contrary to natural desires and wishes.
For nearly two weeks I have been suffering from a
very painful disease and am now in hospital here.

    It is now nearly two years and a half since I
began to live my present sinful life, and all that
time I have been cruelly oppressed and mercilessly
treated under my master, an iron-hearted tyrant.
Two weeks ago my disease was very painful, and
I asked my master to send me to a doctor, but
instead of that he treated me worse than ever. I
am now really outcast and thrown in the depths of
great disappointment and despair. It seems as if
there is nobody to help me.

    On the 18th of last month I sent for my
mother and ran away from the house of the tyrant

without his knowledge, but unfortunately I was caught and taken back the next evening. I cannot go out at all, not even to the bath, and not only that, but they do not give me sufficient food. My present condition is worse than that of a slave. My liberty is taken from me altogether.

I felt so oppressed and sorrowful, that I decided to commit suicide, but when I began to think of my poor mother and that she would be left alone and helpless in the world, I hesitated to kill myself and gave up my foolish intention.

I heard lately of your Rescue Home and that you are ready to help girls who sincerely give up a life of sin. I do pray that your earnest, warm sympathy and kind help may be given me. I really hope to escape from the hand of the oppressor as soon as I can, and live a righteous, happy, free life. Have mercy on me and deliver me.

Yours, _____

I went down to Kobe to help this girl, but she was removed to Kyoto. We followed her there and succeeded in securing her release, though not without considerable difficulty and great risk. I took her to our Tokyo Home, and she was afterwards converted, and got married and comfortably settled.

Those days were full of exciting happenings in which officers manifested the greatest devotion and courage. Lt. Commissioner Yamamuro, Brigadier Yabuki, Brigadier Hatcher, and others, in response to appeals sent to us, went to towns far removed from the railway, and at very great personal risk, succeeded in obtaining the release of girls and brought them to our Rescue Home.

The excitement throughout the nation continued to increase, until the Government was obliged to take action. They did so in a manner characteristic of the thoroughness of the Japanese people. They took a course that could only be followed in a supreme national emergency--the issue of an Imperial Ordinance prepared by the Ministers of State and signed by the Emperor, which had the full force of law. This course could, however, only be adopted when Parliament was not in session and circumstances made immediate action absolutely imperative. The terms of the Ordinance provided that any girl who desired her liberty to go to the nearest police station, state her desire, and her name would immediately be removed from the register, and she would

be free, without regard to any financial liability to her keepers. It was made a penal offence for any keeper or employee to attempt to hinder any girl wishing to leave.

The issue of this Imperial Ordinance was a result far beyond our most sanguine expectations. It at once threw open the doors of these haunts of vice, and was indeed a most royal proclamation of liberty to the captives. As a result of this change in the law, *over 12,000 young women abandoned their lives of sin during the first year alone,* and returned to their homes and to paths of purity. Great rejoicing took place throughout the Empire. Broken hearts were healed. Thousands of families welcomed home loved ones for whom for years, in many cases, self-sacrificing but futile efforts had been made to secure their release. It removed the outstanding evil effect of a most hateful system, and has for ever made it illegal in Japan to retain any girl and force her to live this life of shame against her will.

This agitation, which revolutionized the system governing prostitution in Japan, is now considered to have been one of the most far-reaching and important events in the national history. Moreover, before this the Army was almost unknown. We were not considered to be worth a paragraph in the daily papers, but as a result of this campaign, the Army became well known and popular throughout the Empire. We were henceforth looked upon as examples of religious zeal--workers of pure and disinterested purpose, toiling with supreme courage and devotion for the people's highest interests. It was a sowing of seed that has produced a glorious harvest and certainly laid the foundations of the God-glorifying work which exists in Japan today.

THE POLLUTION OF PORNOGRAPHY

Excerpted from a series of articles on pornography
in "The War Cry"

Published by
The Salvation Army
National Headquarters
Verona, N.J., USA

Authors included:
Henry Gariepy (August 2, 1986)
James Dobson (July 19, 1986)
Lois Hoadley Dick (June 21, 1986)
An Unnamed Prisoner (October 11, 1986)

1. Salvation Army at War with Pornography
(Henry Gariepy)

PORNOGRAPHY IS A MORAL CANCER eating at the heart of America, with women and children its primary victims. There has been a mushrooming of this literature of deviants that perverts the mind and distorts moral values. We have a responsibility to help protect the innocent from the destructiveness of this epidemic.

The Salvation Army in recent months has stepped up its longstanding war on pornography. Astonishing evidence has recently emerged that indisputably documents that violent sex-related crimes are closely linked to pornography. Psychiatrists, psychologists, sexual abuse therapists, battered wives, molested children, in case after doleful case, have testified to being forced to imitate perverted sexual acts depicted in porn magazines.

Child sexual abuse is fueled by pornography. A *New York Times* article quoted justice authorities in saying, "Thousands of children under 18 years old are killed annually by repeat murderers who prey sexually on children and adults involved in child prostitution and pornography."

Let us stand up and be counted for the support of decency and the elimination of this cancer from our cities and neighborhoods.

2. James Dobson Calls for Anti-Porn Action

The explosive growth of pornography in the U.S. will be curbed when citizens demand action, according to Dr. James Dobson. Dobson, noted Christian author and family therapist, served on the U.S. Attorney General's Commission on Pornography during the past year. In a letter to his supporters, Dobson reflected on his involvement with the commission and called for action against obscenity.

Calling his commission involvement "the most difficult and unpleasant experience of my professional life," Dobson said he was exposed to pornography "far more perverse and wicked" than the "air-brushed nudity in today's mens' magazines."

"Indeed," he wrote, "the mainstream of explicit material sold in sex shops today focuses on rape, incest, defecation, urination, mutilation, bestiality, vomiting, enemas, homosexuality and sadomasochistic activity. Even child pornography, which is illegal and not available over the counter, continues to thrive in a multimillion dollar black market. It is produced by pedophiles for use by other pedophiles in the sexual exploitation of children. Obscenity is a wretched business, top to bottom." Dobson criticized government officials for showing "a complete disregard for the plague of pornography which grips our land." He particularly condemned "permissive judges who have refused to punish the occasional pornographers who were convicted. It has not been uncommon," he said, "for producers earning millions in illicit profits to receive fines of $100 or less. Prison sentences have seldom been handed down, even to the most flagrant offenders."

Dobson cited eight dangers of pornography that he had come to recognize during his year-long study of obscenity:

- widespread depictions of women as victims of violence leads men to believe women really want to be abused;
- the use of pornography seems to be "addictive and progressive" in nature;
- pornography is reaching children who "may never enjoy healthy attitudes about sex" as a result;
- pornography is "degrading and humiliating to women";

- it is used by pedophiles to "soften children's defenses against sexual exploitation";
- outlets for obscenity attract sex-related crimes, as well as prostitution, narcotics and street crime;
- "so-called adult bookstores often become cesspools of disease and homosexual activity";
- pornography is damaging to the family.

The commission's report included several hundred pages of specific recommendations, said Dobson, but "aggressive action against pornographers will not occur unless our citizens demand the response of government ... our commission report will either become another expensive dust collector on bureaucratic shelves or it will serve as the basis for a new public policy. The difference will be determined by the outcry that accompanies the report--or the deafening silence of an unconcerned populous."

3. Pornography's Victims (Lois Hoadley Dick)

Pornography has been called the victimless crime. Does it hurt anyone, this $4 billion-a-year business? Is it anyone's concern what consenting adults do in private? Does one adult bookstore mean the whole neighborhood will soon go down the moral drain?

Most people are *opposed* to pornography and its sister, prostitution, but they have not been *exposed* to it. Because of their ignorance they lack the righteous anger they should feel.

Pornography is in no way a victimless crime. The most pitiable victims are children, American boys and girls and young teens. Thirty thousand of them, runaways, pour yearly into the Times Square area of Manhattan, and 60 percent are funneled directly into the porno or prostitution business.

Children as young as 5 and 6 are solicited off the streets by "chicken hawks" who haunt the bus terminals and railroad stations. According to the founder of a rescue mission there, the pornographers starve, rape, and otherwise abuse their young captives. He blames public apathy for the appalling situation.

"I'm sure everybody takes advantage of children at some time or another," an old wreck of a man whined to a reporter. The old man maintained a mailing list of fifty thousand names for his kiddie porn business before his arrest and sentence to a penitentiary for molesting children.

A veteran policeman of thirty years service in the Pittsburgh area described his shock after a raid on a kiddie porn ring: "Whips, boots, handcuffs, masks and paddles were confiscated. Also, an 11-year-old boy worked as a procurer to recruit little girls."

The pornography business threatens our future as a nation, and our very humanity. Yet Christians close their minds to what they don't want to know.

Child pornography lives off the bodies of kids. If a child loses his self-respect and morality he has nothing left. There are fifty grisly tot murders a year associated with the prostitution industry in New York City alone. Children are beheaded, thrown from rooftops, found dead with multiple stab wounds.

Men tourists are approached by a familiar personage: "Come in and see the show. I can get you any little boy or girl you want for 25 dollars a half-hour."

There is nothing more addicting than pornography. No one who understands the raw facts dares to call pornography a victimless crime.

4. Doing Time for Rape (Letter from a Prisoner)

I'd like you to know just how important it is to me to join The Salvation Army's war on pornography.

I personally know just what effect pornography can have on the mind of a man who is addicted. I know because I'm doing time for rape. This is the result of my addiction to pornography.

I started out quite innocently. I was 15 years old when I found nude photos my Dad thought he'd kept hidden from us boys. As I got older, the more I became involved in pornography, especially because it became more accessible.

Eventually, I had to live out the fantasies I received when I watched the triple "X" movies. I was arrested and charged for serious sex offenses and weapons possession.

I do not justify my crimes. I thank God I now know what caused me to do it. Most helpful to me is the close relationship I've found with my Saviour. I didn't know Christ on the street. Now He's my dearest friend and I thank God for Him.

Please tell your readers that when pornography addiction leads to crime, the immediate victims are not the only victims. Consider the pain suffered by the attacker's wife and children. The attacker himself is also a victim because he's not aware he's addicted.

Pornography is as addictive as alcohol and drugs and should be outlawed. I don't feel the First Amendment was intended to permit publication of materials that are designed to destroy human lives. That is exactly what pornography does.

You may be assured I personally wish to do all I can to help you win your war against pornography.

A FIGHT WITH THE DRAGON

(Full Title: A Fight in 1885 with the Dragon for Innocence and Purity)

By Bramwell Booth

From "The Staff Review"

Published by
The Salvation Army
International Headquarters
London (October 1924)

In the autumn of 1885 I was indicted at the Old Bailey--the Central Criminal Court of the United Kingdom--together with the late W. T. Stead, then editor of *The Pall Mall Gazette,* and certain other persons, on the charge of unlawfully taking Eliza Armstrong, aged thirteen, out of the possession of her parents and against her will. The other persons concerned in the alleged abduction were Rebecca Jarrett, a woman who had formerly kept a house of ill-fame, and had reformed her life after coming under the influence of The Salvation Army; Elizabeth Combe, a Swiss officer of the Army; and Mussabini, a Greek who had taken the name of Sampson Jacques, and had assisted Stead in the investigations. There was a further charge against Stead, Jarrett, and Jacques, together with Madame Mourez, a procuress, of being concerned in an assault on the child in question.

The case was tried before Mr. Justice Lopes and a common jury. Mr. Justice Lopes, who afterwards became Lord Ludlow, was said to have exceptional ability in a certain class of case, but not even his closest legal friend would claim a place for him among the great lawyers of his time.

Any distinction which the bench lacked, however, was fully made up in the well of the court. The then Attorney-General, Sir Richard Webster, who afterwards became Lord Alverstone and Lord Chief Justice of England, led the prosecution for the Crown, and with him were Mr. (now Sir Harry) Poland and Mr. R. S. Wright, then M.P. for Norwich, and afterwards a very able judge of the Queen's Bench.

On our side another future Lord Chief, then simply Mr. Charles Russell, appeared for Rebecca Jarrett. He was the outstanding figure in the defense, and showed the conspicuous qualities for which the name of Lord Russell of Killowen will long be remembered in the annals of bench and bar. His junior was Mr. Charles Matthews, afterwards Public Prosecutor. My own counsel was Mr. S. D. Waddy, Q.C., later a judge of the County Court, and with him were Mr. Horne Payne and Mr. R. F. Colam. Mr. Sutherst was for Mrs. Combe, while Jacques's principal counsel was Mr. Henry Matthews, who became Home Secretary in Lord Salisbury's Government, and afterwards was raised to the peerage as Viscount Llandaff.

Stead defended himself, though his case was "watched" by Charles Matthews.

The hearing occupied thirteen days in all, and seldom if ever can the Old Bailey have witnessed the unfolding of such a drama. The facts which were elicited created a profound sensation throughout the country, and, indeed, in many parts of the world. In the result I was acquitted; the charge against Elizabeth Combe was dismissed before the case for the defense was even opened; Stead was found guilty of abduction and of aiding and abetting in the assault, and was sentenced to three months' imprisonment; Jacques was acquitted on the first charge, but was found guilty on the same offense as Stead on the second, and was sentenced to one month's imprisonment, and Jarrett was found guilty on both charges and sentenced to six months' imprisonment. In all these cases the punishment was without hard labor, but Madame Mourez, whose case was in a different category, was sentenced to imprisonment with hard labor for six months.

Behind this prosaic narration of names and facts is a somewhat important episode in the social history of modern England. The trial itself was an anti-climax; it was a cross-scent on the trail, and although, as I will explain presently, it had its uses, particularly for The Salvation Army, it must not occupy the field of exclusion of the real achievement, namely the violent awakening of the public conscience which had already taken place on the subject of child prostitution, and the expression of that conscience in the passing of the Criminal Law Amendment Act of 1885.

I am concerned mainly in these pages with my own and the Army's share in the events of those agitating days, and I write simply from that point of view.

From our earliest years as the Christian Mission there came, occasionally, to our penitent-form in Whitechapel, unfortunate girls who looked to us for some means of enabling them to throw off the fetters of their deadly calling. Here and there kind women-comrades would fix up these poor creatures for a night or two, but that was only a very casual and uncertain method of dealing with the problem.

Presently one motherly woman, a baker's wife, who had already given up her front room to Magdalen, suggested to me that if only she had more accommodations she could take in these girls for a few days and look after them until they were passed on to some employment. Accordingly, the Army helping her, she and her husband took a larger cottage, which was soon given over entirely to this work, and another cottage was taken in addition. The name of Mrs. Cottrill, in her little home in a shabby East End street, is one to be handed down in honor to our Army posterity, not only for what she herself did, but for the mighty rescue work to which it led. To such humble souls there is reared no monument on earth, save the work of which they help to lay the foundations, but surely there is a window set up in Heaven!

This work in which the Army, without any set purpose of its own, was gradually led in this way, was placed under the personal supervision of Mrs. Bramwell Booth. Some time after my marriage the General, talking with me of this new development, had said, "What about Florrie?" (meaning my wife). "She is very young, I know, but if she feels her heart drawn in that way, then let her have charge." From this time forward my wife began to interest herself in these pitiful cases, and she was duly appointed to lead the new undertaking.

Before she had been at her task for six months, it was brought home to her that a frightful state of things existed in London. She was prepared for the evidence of widespread prostitution, terrible as that is, but it came upon her as an appalling revelation to find that young girls--children, really, of thirteen and fourteen--were being entrapped by a vicious network of carefully devised agencies and in their innocence condemned to a life of shame. She declared further that there existed a regular traffic in these girls; that it had widespread ramifications, both in England and on the Continent; that it was maintained by the most atrocious fraud and villainy, and involved such anguish and degradation, as, in her opinion, could not be matched by any trade in human beings known to history.

Those hideous facts greatly affected her, and during the first year or two of our married life the skies were often overcast on this account. Where there should have been smiles and brightness there were often tears and sorrow. Thinking of the miseries of these poor creatures, Mrs. Booth cried herself to sleep night after night. She told me of the most harrowing incidents which had come to her knowledge. I tried to comfort her by suggesting that the stories were probably exaggerated, that the credibility of these folks was not to be trusted too readily, and so on. But, presently yielding to her entreaties, I said that I would look into the matter for myself. I made certain inquiries and interviewed one or two people. Among the latter was the then Chamberlain of the City of London, Mr. Benjamin Scott, who, in association with Mrs. Josephine Butler, had been attacking the Contagious Diseases Acts then in force. He said that he could well believe all that I heard from my wife, that it was a disgrace to civilization, and that some of the police winked at the betrayers and procurers. He expressed in his gentle, courteous way the hope that something would be done. I answered him with emphasis that something would!

* * * *

It was some little time after this that, on arriving at our offices in Queen Victoria Street one day, I was informed that the housekeeper when he opened the front gate at seven o'clock that morning had found a young girl outside who had told him an extraordinary story. The girl, a decent, well-favored girl of about seventeen, wearing a very beautiful red silk dress, was brought to me. She told me that she had come up from the country to London in answer to an advertisement for a girl to help in the general work of a house, and had been received on arrival by the mistress who had answered her application. She soon found, however, that she had been entrapped into a brothel. As the days went on her "mistress" urged her with increasing force to be a "lady" like the others in the house, gave her the red silk dress, and compelled her to visit a certain music-hall in her company. The girl resisted all importunities, but escape seemed to be impossible, and she did not know what to do or where to go.

On the previous night a man had made himself very objectionable, whereupon she fled and barricaded herself in one of the kitchens, yielding neither to threats nor cajolery. After some time she heard the landlady say, "Leave her there till morning; she will come to her senses when she wants her breakfast." Left alone, the girl remembered amid her alarm and agitation that in her own town she had attended some meetings of The Salvation Army, and that in her box was an old song book, which bore on its cover the address of General Booth. He was surely the one person in all the great city who would help her!

It was four o'clock in the morning before everything was still in the house. She waited a while and then crept up to her room, found the little red-covered song book and slipped out. Inquiring her way of a policeman, she walked from Pimlico to Queen Victoria Street, and remained outside the door of headquarters until it was opened.

The story was hard to believe, but there was the girl, who had been found outside the door between seven and eight o'clock that morning; and there, moreover, was the dress, which obviously was not such as a mistress would provide for a domestic servant.

I sent a man at once to her address from which she said that she had escaped. There they stated at first they knew nothing of her, but when he told them that they were telling lies, and that he was an officer of The Salvation Army, which already had the girl under its protection, they changed their tune. At last he got her box away, and we found further confirmation of her story.

The incident made a great impression upon me, an impression which was deepened further when a number of girls were brought up from Whitechapel by Mrs. Booth, and I had the opportunity of questioning them. One of them, about fourteen years old, manifestly *enceinte*, told a terrible story of how she had been met in the street by a very "nice" woman, taken to a music-hall, persuaded to meet her "friend" again, and so dragged into virtual imprisonment and the last outrage.

It was during the agonies of that time that I resolved-- and recorded my resolve on paper--that, no matter what the consequences might be, I would do all I could to stop the abominations, to rouse public opinion, to agitate for the improvement of the law, to bring to justice the adulterers and the murderers, and to make a way of escape for the victims.

It will be asked: Where, all this time, were the police? Was there no law which could be invoked to scourge the offenders? The legislative position in 1885 was this: The House of the Lords, to its credit, had already three times passed a Bill the primary object of which was to ensure greater protection for young girls and women, and particularly to raise the age at which a girl's consent could free her seducer from responsibility. The age at that time, wickedly and absurdly, was thirteen! On the first two occasions the Bill, after passing the Upper House, met with some untimely fate in the Lower. It was passed for the third time by the Lords in the spring of this fateful year. We knew that the Government was very tepid on the whole question, and without the stimulus of popular agitation it seemed unlikely that the Bill would meet with any greater success on its third venture into the House of Commons than on its first or second. As a matter of fact, to anticipate a little, although Sir William Harcourt, whom we approached, lost no time in putting the Bill on the Orders of the House, it was talked out on the second reading in early May. Altogether an inglorious chapter in the records of the People's Chamber!

The appeal, then, must be to the people themselves, whose heart and conscience, we were sure, had not been interpreted by their representatives in Parliament assembled.

*　*　*　*

After some further conference with various friends, including Benjamin Scott and Mrs. Josephine Butler, I consulted W. T. Stead, and told him the facts of child enslavement and prostitution as they had come to our notice. I said that I and Mrs. Booth had looked into them sufficiently to feel that, although there might, here and there, be exaggerations, there was urgent need for the passing and strengthening, if possible, of the measure then before Parliament. I asked him to give publicity to the business so that the Government should become aware of the pressure of public opinion.

At first Stead hesitated. He had not been so very long in London, and though the Editor of *The Pall Mall Gazette*, was not perhaps so firmly in the saddle as afterwards. Finally, however, he came to headquarters; I introduced him there to Benjamin Scott, who explained the legal situation and also the Continental traffic, a branch of the iniquity with the history and details of which Scott was specially familiar. After Scott had gone, I told Stead that I had three or four women in the next room, together with a converted brothel-keeper, whom he might interview for himself. These women were brought in one by one, and Stead put them through their stories. Women, I call them, but, with the exception of Rebecca Jarrett, they were all under sixteen.

When the interrogatories were ended and the girls had withdrawn, there was a pause and I looked at Stead. He was evidently deeply moved by what he had heard. It had shaken his vehement nature, and presently his feelings found vent. Raising his fist, he brought it down on my table with a mighty bang, so that the very inkpots shivered, and he uttered one word, the word "DAMN!" This explosion over, I said, "Yes, that is all very well, but it will not help us. The first thing to do is to get the facts in such a form that we can publish them." Stead agreed; we not only took counsel together, we prayed together, and then he went away.

A period of consideration and hesitation followed. Ultimately we had another meeting at headquarters and decided that the best thing to do would be to examine the situation, independently of the evidence of the injured girls which we had collected.

Stead wanted to obtain first-hand information. I provided a woman who actually went and placed herself in a brothel as though she were a woman of doubtful character, and lived there for ten days, reporting what happened. This beautiful and fearless girl carried through the scheme with complete satisfaction. We provided her with money, so that she could pay the brothel-keeper suitably and at the same time express a certain fastidiousness with regard to callers. Although she had some unpleasant experiences, she came through unharmed.

We planned also that Stead should visit her in the house, and there she told him that awful story of what she had witnessed concerning girls of thirteen and thereabouts. Other people also were set upon the task of investigation, including a detective, a clever fellow, the Greek already mentioned. In the result we found a great deal more immorality in London than we had ever supposed to exist, a great many more houses of ill-fame than even the police had known about, but, shocking and sorrowful as all this was, it concerned men and women, and was more or less open and acknowledged.

The further thing which we found, and the discovery of which determined our subsequent action, was that running through all this brazen organization of vice, was, as Mrs. Booth had affirmed, a deeper and darker vein of more cruel and appalling wickedness--nothing less than a traffic in children who were lured to a physical and moral doom. It was not the immorality that stung us so much, horrible as it was: it was the deliberate scheming and planning whereby young girls, often mere children, were bought and sold as irrevocably as in a slave market.

The *Pall Mall Gazette* "Extra" of July 6, 1885, in which Stead described "The Maiden Tribute of Modern Babylon," took the British public by storm in a way that can hardly be paralleled in newspaper history. I remember that I was out of London on the afternoon that the first article, which I had already seen in proof, appeared, and, returning in the evening, I found that the only copies of *The Pall Mall Gazette* to be obtained were being sold by boys in Ludgate Circus for half-a-crown a sheet. The sensation was all the more tremendous because *The Pall Mall Gazette* had a high reputation for exactitude. It was a paper of tone and privilege, much patronized by clubmen. The hot waves of public feeling quickly swelled and lapped up to the doors of the House of Commons.

On the very day of the publication of the first of the articles Lord Salisbury's new Ministry had met Parliament. Sir Michael Hick-Beach, in his program for the remainder of the session, had made no reference to the Criminal Law Amendment Bill, which had been left in the air--and, being House of Commons air, none too healthy a medium to be suspended in. Nor did the ex-Ministers opposite protest against the omission. But a day or two later, evidently prompted by the state of feeling outside, the Home Secretary, Sir Richard Cross, proposed to resume the interrupted debate, on a promise of co-operation from Sir William Harcourt. Stead and I and one or two propagandists were called in to suggest how the measure could be strengthened. The Bill was a week in Committee in the House of Commons, and it passed into law early in August. The age of consent was put even higher than the fifteen years on which the Lords had insisted. On the motion of the Home Secretary himself, by 179 votes to 71, it was raised to sixteen. Never has there been a more immediate capitulation to the Fourth Estate. But the Fourth Estate in this case had behind it a British public stirred to the depths.

* * * *

The events--and the triumph--I have here narrated will raise the query, "Why the Old Bailey? Why three months' imprisonment for the chivalrous man who had laid bare the infamy, and in doing so had risked his reputation and even his life? Why imprisonment, or at least the strain and odium of public trial, for his associates?" Strange indeed it was that in the first case of any public interest under the new Criminal Law Amendment Act the "criminals" in the dock should be, not the monsters who had battened on the villainy, but the men and women who had helped to expose it! To explain that strange twisting of causes and circumstances, I must retrace my steps a little, and go back to the secret inquiry which led to the publication of the "Maiden Tribute."

It was one thing for Stead and the rest of us to satisfy ourselves of the truth of the position; it was another thing to gain public credence for what who knew. It was not enough to put forward the general results of our observations; we must have concrete cases proved or capable beyond all doubt of being proved. Before venturing on publication, therefore, Stead suggested that certain experiments be made. He got an old procuress to "sell" him two girls, both under sixteen, for each of whom he paid £10.

The girls were produced at the appointed house, and Stead had a talk with each of them with the object of discovering how far they were aware of the nature of the transaction. It was evident, particularly so in the case of one of them, that they had only the vaguest notion of any possible impropriety. Stead's blunt talk thoroughly frightened them, however, and, giving each of them £5, he sent them away. Other experiments of various kinds were made, equally confirmatory of what we had heard.

But even such stories were not definite enough for the purpose. They would have to be taken only on the word of Stead and those co-operating with him. We then decided that the only other thing to do was to make an experiment with an actual case, and to carry it through in such a way that we could call evidence from people of repute with regard to what had happened. We thought the plan out most carefully, and it was put into execution on the Derby day of 1885.

The plan was this: that Rebecca Jarrett, who, being an ex-brothel-keeper, understood the business, should go to some woman whom she knew would part with her child. The child should be taken to a professional procuress (Madame Mourez), who would certify it to be a *virgo intacta*, this being one of the abominations essential to such transactions. Then it was arranged that the child should be conveyed to a well-known house where Stead had engaged a room, and that there he should be left alone with her for an hour or so. It was important, further, to have it certified after this experience, that nothing had happened to the child, and accordingly it was agreed that she should be taken from the brothel by one of our trusted women who was a great benefactor in these investigations, and was known throughout as Mrs. X., straight to the home of a specialist whose name I had suggested, and who had most warmly agreed to help us, and that the specialist, after examining her, should furnish a certificate.

All this was done to plan, and the next morning at Charing Cross Station I received the child from Jarrett, and Mrs. Combe conveyed her to Paris. Thus the case was proved up to the hilt, for although this particular girl had received no whit of harm, it was shown to be possible for a procuress to buy a child for money, to certificate her, bring her to a house of ill-fame, introduce her to a man she had never seen before, ruin her, and send her off to the Continent so that nothing further need be known of her.

The moment this was done, Stead felt that his case was complete. He already had his information; he simply wanted to clinch it. The exposures in *The Pall Mall Gazette* soon followed.

It would have been wonderful in such an enterprise if there had been no mistakes or miscalculations. The mistakes never made me regret in the least the plan that we pursued. The need was desperate, and was met by desperate measures, which usually mean risk. The little circumstance which led us eventually to the dock was the (quite unnecessary) publication by Stead of a letter which the girl had written from France to her mother, and which, of course, had been intercepted. He published it with the object of showing the innocence of the child who had been sold for money.

In this letter she had quoted a childish rhyme, which her mother recalled that she knew, and at once said, "That's my Eliza" (the child had been called by another name in the revelations). Forthwith, in the character of the injured parent, she went to a great enemy of ours who did not like the prominence which The Salvation Army had obtained through the affair. Another story was also set before the editor of a Sunday newspaper, also no friend to the Army. The "crime" stood revealed! The girl had been abducted! We, the protagonists of repressive legislation, had broken our own law! An evening rival of *The Pall Mall*--now defunct--took the case up. Information was laid on which a charge could be preferred. We were summoned under our own Act, which, of course provided for much heavier sentences than had been possible under the old law! We, a gang of subterranean engineers, were hoist with our own petard!

The circumstances of the trial at the Old Bailey need not be gone into at any length. Stead and I and the others were summoned in the first instance to appear at Bow Street, and a warrant was issued for the arrest of Rebecca Jarrett; I had refused to disclose her whereabouts, fearing, as I did, that, her case being on a somewhat different plane from ours, she might be refused bail. We resolved that we would not have her arrested until the trial, when we hoped to be able to get bail for her along with ourselves, and so it turned out.

Every blackguard in London must have assembled in Bow Street while the case was before the magistrate. From every foul den in the metropolis the people had come to gloat on the discomfiture of these modern Galahads. I was mobbed more than once, dragged out of a cab, and maltreated, and only rescued with difficulty by a police inspector who drove the crowd right and left. On more than one occasion the police placed a "Black Maria" at our disposal, and we were rapidly conveyed from the Court to some distant Square where cabs could be available for us.

And, apart from the mob who shook *our* heads, there were the righteous and respectable people who shook their own. They were agreed as to the evil, were, in fact, horrified that such things could happen in their midst, but, with here and there an exception, they strongly disapproved our methods of meeting it. It was impossible to disapprove of theirs, because they gave no hint of having any.

And so to the Old Bailey. Here the feeling inside and outside the Court was intense. At times during the hearing, the Court was very subdued, the common hush almost suggesting a religious solemnity; at other times there was outburst and clamor. The public excitement could not be kept away from the precincts of the law. I am bound to say that on the whole we were personally treated with consideration. The robing room was given up to us, and we lunched together. Everything that could be unpleasant was dispensed with, except the necessary formality of locking us up for a few minutes in the cells each morning before we entered the dock. I had the "condemned" cell, by the way, not, I am sure, because of its associations, but because it happened to be the most commodious in the Old Bailey. The warders were very civil, the police quite nice, and all the time we were sustained by a current of friendliness, if not of sympathy, even on the part of some who were against us.

Mr. Justice Lopes, who behaved with great civility to me personally, was against us from the beginning. His view was evidently that we were all guilty. He showed himself particularly hostile at first, but weakened considerably, and it was at his suggestion that Mrs. Combe was released, long before the hearing concluded. All parties agreed that there was no evidence against her, meaning, of course, that they had not been able to secure any evidence.

Rebecca Jarrett broke down under cross-examination. She had kept a house of ill-fame, and certain things were brought forward relating to her past which she had not the courage to admit. It was a cruel ordeal for her, and I repented while I sat in the dock listening to her in the witness-box that I had allowed her to embark on such an adventure. Yet I am satisfied that the evidence we obtained through her was an essential link in the chain, and that without it we should never have enforced the need for raising the age.

My own feelings during the summing-up are set down in a letter written to my mother from the dock; from which I make an extract:

> As to the case, I have no regrets as to what I did. The mistakes and accidents all through have only been such as are usually attached to all human enterprises. I regret them, but I could not prevent them, glad as I would have been to do so. It is painful to have all regard for motive shut out of what they think it well to shut it out from, and yet to imply all sorts of bad motives in connection with the smallest incidents of the affair. But I beg of you not to be distressed in any way about me personally. God will take care of me!

> Then another thing. I hope that no efforts will be made on my behalf, if we go to prison, that are not made on behalf of Stead. Do please let me beg this of you....

The jury showed a very intelligent mastery of the problem. Although we were told over and over again as the trial proceeded that motive had nothing to do with the law, and that the simple question was whether or not we had abducted the girl, we could see day by day that the jury were coming more and more to the conviction that motive must be allowed for.

They were almost bound to find Stead guilty because of his own admissions, technical though they were, yet such was their evident hesitation in doing so, and such the volume of public sentiment outside, that Mr. Justice Lopes gave what was a comparatively light sentence--three months--which the Home Secretary promptly ordered should be in the first division. Still, it was a conviction, and my satisfaction in my own acquittal was overshadowed by it.

The feature of the whole trial, in my opinion, was Charles Russell's speech for Jarrett. It was one of his most wonderful efforts. He spoke for two hours, and when he sat down, my dear wife sent up a note to me in the dock saying that she did not care how the case ended after that speech! "It was worth it all." Although Rebecca Jarrett in her evidence had produced an unfavorable impression, yet when Russell finished speaking for her there was not a dry eye in the Court. Even the Judge and the Clerk of Arraigns were moved by the appeal which he made on her behalf. When the Attorney-General came to reply, he dealt with Rebecca very cautiously.

During his cross-examination, Sir Richard Webster showed some tendency to bully. One of his favorite methods in cross-examining was to repeat the question, "Do I understand you to say...?" At last I said to him in reply to one such repetition, "Sir Richard, I have told you once. Why do you ask me again?" From that point his manner greatly improved.

One small circumstance which I recall with regard to Webster was our discovery of a bundle of letters on the table of the apartment assigned to our use, which Webster had evidently mislaid. I took them up and read one or two, thinking they were ours, but finding that they belonged to the prosecuting counsel, sent them to him. I gathered enough of their contents to know that they were letters from his constituents--he had just been elected for Launceston--hotly criticizing him for appearing against The Salvation Army!

The best speech after Russell's was Waddy's for me. Both Russell and Waddy saw our position from the beginning, but certain of our legal friends misunderstood it in some respects. At one of the conferences in the

Temple, at which nearly all the counsel--a formidable array--engaged in the defense were present, Stead expressed our unwillingness to take a certain line which, though it might be useful for the defense, was not, in his opinion, entirely candid. Thereupon Henry Matthews, in the presence of us all, burst out with the exclamation, "Oh, Russell, I cannot stand these people's thirst for being martyrs!" Stead replied like lightning, "No! you will never be one." It was the idea of some of these gentlemen in wigs that the whole thing was a flare, either to win renown for The Salvation Army, or to make the fortune of a newspaper.

* * * *

The uses to the trial? Of course, we had already obtained the Act, and we counted nothing else of very much moment. But the trial did the Army a great deal of good. It made us known and put us at one stroke in the very front rank of those who were contending for a better treatment of the lost and the poor; and while it roused some powerful enemies, especially in the Press, the enmity lasted only for a time, while the sympathy which was generated remained and remains a permanent possession.

Our work for women was greatly furthered by these strange circumstances. We gained friends in the political circles, won recognition from the Government then existing and from its successors, and were brought into touch with Queen Victoria and with some of her Court who ever since have been interested in what we have been doing. We knew from the Dowager Marchioness of Ely and others that the Queen followed the proceedings with great concern and sympathy.

The case opened doors for us also in the oversea Dominions, and in the United States, and the sympathy materialized in financial help, which, if not at the time large in amount, was encouraging in character.

A word may be said on subsequent happenings as they concern one or two of the persons who figured in these proceedings. One strange circumstance was the discovery, ten years later, that Eliza Armstrong was the illegitimate daughter of the woman who had posed as the injured mother. Had this been known at the time it is very improbable that we should have been prosecuted at all. The Salvation Army has since assisted Eliza more or less. The mention of Rebecca Jarrett shall close this episode. It is pleasant to record that she has done well. Her subsequent life has amply proved the sincerity of her repentance. She is still under the care of the Army, enjoying a happy old age, free from the bondage of the past, and trying to serve God in the sphere in which He has in His mercy placed her.

IV. Crime

William Booth calls this "a black river, indeed." However, he admits, "How imperfect is the prospect we have of any substantial or permanent improvement, either in its volume or the methods employed for dealing with it."

"I have talked," he said, "with men and women, both practical and scientific, who are deeply interested in this subject, in almost every country I have visited, and I have read much of what they have to say on the painful topic, but, how imperfect is their comprehension of its character, and how insufficient the proposals which even the wisest and most practical of them have to make for any modification of the evil, either in quality or quantity."

Then Booth the Evangelist insists that the solution is not merely in better prisons, but in the reclamation of the prisoners. He declares:

> "Those concerned upon the subject will occasionally go so far as to admit that the reclamation of the criminal is more important than the reformation of the prison, desirable as that may be; but outside The Salvation Army, and a handful of people who imitate us, you will seldom, if ever, hear anyone insisting upon the necessity of that reclamation being affected through the salvation bought for the criminal, just as much as for any one else, by the sacrifice of Jesus Christ.

> "Conversion is the unfailing remedy. Salvation will make him honest, because he will be a new man; he will make for himself a new world."

Crime (from *Darkest England*)

Our prisons ought to be reforming institutions, which should turn men out better than when they entered their doors. As a matter of fact they are often quite the reverse. (page 181)

The Salvation Army has at least one great qualification for dealing with this question. I believe I am in the proud position of being at the head of the only religious body which has always some of its members in jail for conscience' sake. We are one of the few religious bodies which can boast that many of those who are in our ranks have gone through terms of penal servitude. We therefore know the prison at both ends. (page 182)

A method by which Society professes to attempt the reclamation of the lost is by the rough, rude surgery of the jail. Upon this a whole treatise might be written, but when it was finished it would be nothing more than a demonstration that our prison system has practically missed aiming at that which should be the first essential of every system of punishment.

It is not reformatory, it is not worked as if it were intended to be reformatory. It is punitive, and only punitive. The whole administration needs to be reformed from top to bottom in accordance with this fundamental principle, viz., that while every prisoner should be subjected to the measure of punishment which shall mark a due sense of his crime both to himself and society, the main object should be to rouse in his mind the desire to lead an honest life; and to effect that change in his disposition and character which will send him forth to put that desire into practice. (pages 81-82)

CRIMINALS NO MORE

By Bernard Watson

From "A Hundred Years War"

Published by
Hodder and Stoughton
London (1964)

In India, The Salvation Army encounters different problems. In the days of British rule, an official of the British Colonial Service said to a missionary officer: "I don't know how you live and work among these people; to us they are cattle, just cattle."

"Sir," the officer replied, "to us they are immortal souls."

He shook his head and there was some justification for his skepticism. The Doms, the Nats, the Sansias, Bhatus, Karwals and other tribes had terrorized India from time immemorial, living outside the law, born and reared in utterly amoral traditions, professional thieves, gangsters, even rapists and murderers.

Their children, upon registration at birth, were automatically classified as criminals. Their skill at crime, nurtured from one crooked generation to another, made the efforts of the police ludicrous. In the manner that a burglar would "case the joint," make an innocent call at a home to find the lie of the land, so they would visit the village selling baskets or some such handicraft. Or they might beg, and frequently be received with compassion and aid. Yet they would return at night to steal everything from the homes of the villagers. Watch-dogs would disappear as if by magic from their poor rooms in which they slept.

The immensity of the country and the density of the population made the task of law enforcement impossible.

One man wrote to a police official:

"Sahib, you are a very strong and clever police officer. You have suppressed crime mightily. But, tell me, what has happened to your two good horses? Are they now in the stables? If they have gone, have they been stolen? Then how could that be, seeing they are so well guarded? You are such a clever policeman and you sleep near where they are stabled. Where are your horses now?"

The thief had wrapped the horses' hooves in blankets, and walked the animals out almost literally from under the official's nose. They were never recovered.

Sometimes crime was on a communal scale and had a comic opera about it.

At Gorakpur, city of about 60,000 souls, large numbers of Doms, one of the criminal tribes, were taken to work in gangs during the day, then locked up in *domrakhanas* at night. After roll call the police locked all doors, posted sentries and went wearily to their quarters. But locks, bolts and high walls were as nothing to men steeped in the lore of centuries of banditry. Moving silently as ghosts, with the keen night vision of the great cats in their jungles, they were busily engaged during the nights in the homes of the sleeping citizenry of Gorakpur.

In the morning they would be awakened by the gong, all present and correct. Naturally the crime rate for Gorakpur was highly inconsistent. The police spent many anxious hours, made many fruitless journeys, trying to find the thieves who reaped such a rich harvest in the city. Meanwhile they kept close guard over the Doms.

Asked why they must thieve they would say that it was because their ancestors had been dispossessed of their land, yet when they were given land they let or sold it.

"We have no bullocks with which to plow," would be their complaint. When they were given bullocks they sold them and pocketed the money.

"The bullocks are no use to us, we have no seed to sow," was their excuse. Provided with seed they ground it for flour, made it into bread and continued with a way of life that appealed to them--terrorizing large areas of the country and resisting all efforts to make decent citizens of them.

In 1908 The Salvation Army was given the task of rehabilitating as many as possible. A chain of agricultural settlements was established all over India in which farming, weaving and various other employments went side by side with schools for the children and Salvation Army halls where it was hoped the "crims" would be persuaded to listen to stories from the Bible and perhaps also learn to pray.

In some cases drastic remedies had to be taken, including the founding of a "Devil's Island" kind of establishment. One group of criminal tribesmen, with their wives and families, were transported to the Andaman Islands in the Bay of Bengal. The men were in chains and Major Edwin Sheard, the Salvation Army officer in charge of the party was advised to carry a gun. He was a man of only moderate stature, quiet and peaceable in disposition.

Of course it would be unthinkable for a Salvation Army officer to be armed, except with faith in God. Sheard, who carried no gun, ordered the manacles to be struck off the legs of the convicts as soon as they arrived at their destination after a 2,000 mile journey. There were dangers, outbursts of anger, threats from the "crims," but there was something about the Sheards, their self-forgetting ministrations, that disarmed the gangsters. The missionaries remained on the Andamans for five years, developing the colony from scratch, for when they arrived not a spade had pierced the soil, not a tree had been cut, not one site surveyed.

In time, the settlement, in Sheard's words, came to be "not unlike three peaceful English villages." Sheard and his wife trusted God--and the convicts. Sometimes, when the "crims" had axes in their hands, the Salvation Army officer could not help remembering that the known crime record of his "family" stood at 300 robberies and fifty murders. Eight of his men had been sentenced to death. His cook was a murderer, three of the village policeman were convicts, the headman of the villages had crime records longer than Major Sheard's arm.

Yet, as the days went by, the "crims" responded to the simple and transparent Christian love of the Salvationists. On Sunday, when the bell tolled its call to worship, groups of orderly, smiling Indians would be seen going in family groups to the Salvation Army hall where the Major would lead the service. What all the might of law, what two centuries of British rule had failed to achieve, a soft-spoken Salvationist had achieved--without a revolver.

Sir John Hewett, Lt. Governor of the United Provinces, first approached The Salvation Army with a request that it attempt to carry out redemptive work among the criminal tribes. Afterwards he said: "I am, however, convinced that in time The Salvation Army will succeed in the object it has in view, namely the absorption of the criminal tribes into the ordinary population. When that has been done, Commissioner Booth-Tucker and those who work with him will have combined to achieve one of the greatest moral redemptions the world has ever seen."

Succeed it did. But the Criminal Tribes Act was rescinded almost immediately India assumed control of its own destinies in 1947. Then when is a "crim" not a "crim"? Can he be redeemed by act of Parliament?

Congress thought so. Certainly there were social causes: gross poverty, injustice, maladministration and numerous other reasons why crime became a way of life for so many people. Social historians will long argue it out, while those who are freed from the heredity stigma of crime by legislation are still people.

At Stuartpuram, near Bapatla, for example, one of The Salvation Army's largest agricultural settlements, members of the Yerikulas were established on a criminal tribes colony in 1914. The land was swamp or poor sandy soil, 3,000 acres of it at the foot of the Eastern Ghats. Much of this was reclaimed and, as one generation followed another, as the day schools and Sunday schools achieved their aims, as literacy increased and the Christian program of the Salvationists bore fruit, there came into existence a huge and fertile communal farm. The desert rejoiced, the former "crims" learned the way of holiness, the rice crops flourished where the wilderness had been.

The Salvation Army does not work by law enacted. A soul is a soul, whether it resides in a burglar or a solid, respectable member of the community. The people who had descended to the plains like the hordes of the Great Khan, and then fled to the mountain with their loot, were Salvationists now, or at least law-abiding citizens, born into Salvationist communities.

What any self-respecting social agency dreads had happened. The residue of Yerikulas, the one-time "crims," had become "institutionalized." They were free to go, but they chose to stay. They had no place in modern times, the poor needy outcasts, the "crims" of 1914. Congress said that they were free, just like any other Indian national and that the British Raj had sinned in labelling groups of people as wrong-doers.

Maybe so, but The Salvation Army could not wash its hands of the people at Stuartpuram because they are reformed and, in many instances, Christianized. It, too, must demonstrate that it can move with the new laws, march on with the times.

The thousands of acres of land at Stuartpuram had become expensive--about 3,000 rupees an acre (£230). It was worth about 2 annas an acre when the Army acquired it: eight acres for one rupee. Everyone was misled by the discovery that the water beneath the surface of the sandy soil, and in the marshes, was brackish.

Then a Salvation Army officer, a former Straits Settlement planter, proved that below the superficial salt water level was good fresh water, plenty of it. The land rocketed in price. Where peanuts had grown, rice was made to grow, and potatoes, tomatoes, coconut.... The place prospered so much that it had its own railway station and villages sprang up like a wild west town after a gold strike. The men who had been "crims" became policemen, postmen, builders and farmers.

Those who had been watched by the police while they worked in groups akin to the chain-gangs of Mississippi, who had been compelled to go to services at the Salvation Army hall, now attended the corps by choice. They were given travel permits to leave the settlement, or cottages of their own. Men were asked if they would accept employment in the settlement factory and were paid the rate for the job. Then they began to believe that the times were changing.

They read the Bible and liked it, something that millions of "Christian" people find difficulty in doing. With that love of story-telling that characterizes the Indian, one man of the Yerikulas earned renown as a story teller, always from the Bible.

"You take your Bible with you?" an officer asked him, when he returned from one long journey.

"Oh no," he replied, "I know them all by heart." This was not strictly speaking true but he is a diligent student of the great book.

There is a fairy-tale element in this story, a happy-ever-after quality that might make those wary who are versed in gloomy newspaper headlines--yet the most fantastic feature of the tale is to come.

The valuable land at Stuartpuram is being given away to the one-time "crims;" parcels of irrigated, good farmland. There are brick houses now, surrounded by fertile fields. In these live today's farmers who are descended from the terrorists of yesterday. The people who were compelled to go to the Army meetings or risk police displeasure now go because they enjoy the meetings: they want to worship that God of the Christians whom they had accepted as part of a new way of life. There's brass, string and reed music of the sort beloved of Indians, and choruses for all to sing, hand-clapping all the while.

More often than not the leader of the meeting is an Indian, a Salvation Army officer most likely. Speakers are Indian and the intervals are taken by neatly apparelled young people's singing groups.

On Monday these same children will go to school, unlike Shakespeare's schoolboy, neither greasy nor unwilling. They wash fastidiously, though their "crim" ancestors loathed water and were normally verminous. They want to go to school: not to be schooled is the new social stigma in India.

As the children walk they pass rice pools where the plants bend over in the breeze from the Bay of Bengal. Sometimes the children hail men high up in the coconut palms, reaping the highly profitable harvest of those prolific trees. Now and then the boys and girls move aside from their dirt road to let the bullocks go by with their load of hay.

Some are singing the chorus they learned at the Salvation Army meeting yesterday. the language is Telugu:

> *santōsha maina ātma nākun-nadi*
> *nākun-nadi, nākun-nadi.*
> *santōsha maina ātma nākun-nadi*
> *stōtram yēsuku.*

> I've got the joy, joy, joy, joy
> Down in my heart,
> Glory to his name.

You may feel it is all very odd. The British of the time of Clive and Hastings would hardly know what to make of it. Even our own Commissioner Booth-Tucker, who began it in 1882, a man of great compassion, who believed all things were possible in God's name, would doubtless be surprised in his genteel way at the dramatic metamorphosis of the "crims."

As for the Yerikulas, the old-time rogues and vagabonds who believed that India owed them a free and easy living, they would be most astonished of all. If their ghosts are up there in their ancient strongholds, those hills far back from the seashore, then they must marvel as they look down.

Their flesh and blood, honest, hard-working and educated. Those barren acres, fruitful and owned by their descendants. Those Sahibs, the feared and hostile regime, now accepted as friends and brothers. Most unbelievable of all, many of the Yerikulas in *Rakshana Sainyamu*--The Salvation Army. Some of them, Captains, Lieutenants, Majors, drummers, students of the Bible. It is well that the "crims" are safe up there with their ghostly ancestors.

THE SALVATION ARMY IN CORRECTIONAL SERVICES

Excerpted from an unpublished manuscript by
James Tackaberry
Toronto

There can be no question but that The Salvation Army has, since its inception, been concerned about the question of crime and punishment and has addressed itself to that concern in a very practical way. From the earliest days, The Salvation Army has taught, within prison walls, of the redeeming love of Christ. However, it must be noted that the initial ministry in the jails was carried on by Salvationists incarcerated because of their faith in Christ, and the peculiar method chosen to express that faith. In 1890, the Founder expressed this fact when he said, "The Salvation Army has at least one great qualification for dealing with the question of correctional problems." He went on to say, "I believe I am in the proud position of being at the head of the only religious body which has always had some of its members in jail for conscience' sake."

In Canada the first recorded jail meetings were held in London on February 9, 1883. Although many Salvationists in Canada were to spend time in prison because of their involvement with the Army, the first such case had not yet taken place. The meeting in London was thus reported in the *Advertiser*: "A detachment of The Salvation Army, consisting of about twenty soldiers, principally women, made a sudden and determined attack on the jail today, taking Turnkey Kelly so completely by surprise that they had almost finished the opening war-song before he realized the position of affairs. However, after holding a service for the benefit of the female prisoners, they peacefully retired, leaving him once again in quiet possession. It is understood they intend visiting that institution weekly hereafter."

According to Army records, correctional work, in an organized form, dates its beginnings to early in 1883 and places its beginnings in the newly settled land of Australia. A Dr. Singleton had been carrying on a very faithful ministry in that land among the convicts. Shortly after Major Barker, of The Salvation Army arrived, and the Doctor invited the Major to assist him in this work. The Major gladly agreed and was soon sharing in the Gospel ministry in the jails. The Doctor then made available to the Major a small mission in the heart of the worst part of Melbourne. This was to become the first Prison-Gate Home in the Army.

After a while other officers joined the Major in this ministry and were given official recognition to hold meetings in the various institutions and to interview inmates privately in their cells. The authorities provided the officers with a list of inmates due for release and arrangements were made to contact these men and to meet those who wished help upon their discharge. They were then taken to the Prison-Gate Home where they were looked after and given a task to occupy their time until they could find suitable work in the community and once again return to society.

In 1882, William Booth, in speaking to a gathering at Regent Hall in London, England, said: "I believe the time will come when Magistrates will give prisoners seven days at the Mill and three months at The Salvation Army." This prophecy was to see its fulfillment in the development of the chaplaincy to the courts. In Toronto in 1886 Captain Jones, a young woman officer, became the first Canadian officer to visit the courts on a regular basis. In her efforts to seek and save "fallen women" she regularly appeared before the bench pleading that some of these young women be released in her care. When this was done, she would take them to the Rescue Home where they would be cared for until they were ready to make their re-entry into society. In 1887 the *Toronto Globe* reported on the effectiveness of this work: "Captain Jones visited and still visits the worst houses of ill-fame in the city, sometimes alone and sometimes in company with Captain Kelly, and by means of these visits and other visits to the Police Court in the morning the 'Rescue Home' during the first four months only of its existence has been the means of plucking from vice no less than a score of girls."

The year 1890 was a significant year for the development of the Correctional work in many parts of the Army world. This was the year that the Founder's social treatise *In Darkest England and the Way Out* was published. In this widely read and critically acclaimed work, William Booth referred to the matter of dealing with the criminal and also with the correctional situation of that time. These are his words, "Who will give these men a helping hand? What is to be done with them? When the criminal comes out of jail, the whole world is but a press (here referring to an instrument of torture) whose punishment is sharp and cruel indeed."

He made the following comment on the correctional institutions of that day. "Our prisons ought to be reforming institutions, which should turn out men better than when they entered the doors. As a matter of fact they are often quite the reverse."

With the realization that many Salvationists had spent time behind bars the General went on to say, "When a man has been to prison in the best of causes he learns to look at the question of prison discipline with a more sympathetic eye for those who are sent there, even for the worst offenses, than judges and legislators who only look at the prison from the outside. Our people, thank God, have never learned to regard a prisoner as a mere convict. He is ever a human being to them, who is to be cared for and looked after as a mother looks after her ailing child."

In this book the Founder made a proposal to take care of the first offender, to shield him from the contamination of prison life; to be present in the courts to offer accommodation and counselling, to extend the establishment of Prison-Gate Homes, to seek access to jails, to supervise "Tickets of Leave" or Parole, and to find employment for released prisoners. He also made a suggestion that a "Poor Man's Lawyer" should be provided for the indigent, a forerunner of today's Legal Aid.

Whether as a response to the *Darkest England* proposals or as a reaction to indicated need is not certain but in the same year of 1890 The Salvation Army in Canada opened its first Prison-Gate Home. It was located at the corner of Yonge and Eglinton in what was then the Village of Eglinton. The work was commenced by Ensign Dawson, who was to remain in correctional work in Canada for more than fifty years.

An enclosed wagon, painted red, officially named the "Deliverer" but more commonly referred to as the "Red Maria" was provided to transport discharged prisoners to the facility from the jails in the city. A number of industrial shops were established at this home among which were a bakery, which was soon producing 800 loaves a week, a wood-pile which employed eight men during the winter months, a repair shop and a boot and shoe-making department. The products of the latter shop had the letters S.A. imprinted in nails on the soles and were commonplace among the working class of that day. It was not long before other Prison-Gate Homes were opened in Kingston, London and Hamilton.

1893 saw the first officers in Canada being appointed specifically to work in the Police Courts. In the same year the League of Mercy was established in Canada. An announcement published in connection with its commencement stated, "The League of Mercy is now formed for the purpose of visiting the various prisons and hospitals in Toronto and other cities. Will those who have friends or relatives in any of the Prisons or Hospitals in Toronto and would be glad for some member of the League of Mercy to visit them, communicate with Mrs. Booth, at Albert Street, Toronto, marking the letters, League of Mercy." For many years thereafter, the League of Mercy spearheaded an intensive visitation program in the jails across the country.

In 1898 Army officers were invited to conduct worship services at Mercer Institute, a women's jail in Toronto. From that moment on, Salvation Army officers were accepted as equals among the clergy for conducting worship services. It was through the influence of the Army that the first Women's Court was opened in Toronto at about this time. In 1903 the Minister of Justice in Ottawa gave the Army officers access to the five federal penitentiaries then in existence in this country. However, for a number of years prior to this, services were being conducted at the penitentiary in Kingston on a fairly regular basis. It is quite interesting to note that Mrs. Major Blanche Read was the first woman to preach to the inmates at Kingston. A report in *All The World* in 1906 claimed that, at that time, the Army in Canada was conducting regular services in 50 jails and penitentiaries across this land.

It was in this same year that Col. Pugmire, the Secretary for Prison Work in this country, addressed the National Prison Congress in Albany, New York. Among other rather astute observations with regard to correctional work, he made the following comments: "Many and difficult are the problems which have to confront all who have to do with the great prison systems of every civilized country. Punitive measures have very rarely proved themselves to be of a reformatory character. Far more often has it been otherwise; but we venture to say that in the salvation of the criminal lies the crux of the whole matter. The transforming grace of God is the only safeguard against moral degeneracy for every class of sinner."

It was about this time that Brigadier Archibald, formerly a Prison Work officer with The Salvation Army became the first Federal Parole Officer. He had previously established a system of parole supervision under the aegis of the Army, and, the effort proving so successful, he was brought into the federal system to bring into existence the Federal Parole System.

1907 saw the Founder, General William Booth, in Canada on one of his many trips overseas and while in Toronto he visited the Central Prison to conduct a service. He was given a great reception by the prisoners, many of whom were moved to tears by his delineation of the lives of convicts with whom he had come in contact. There was no audience that interested him more, he announced at the outset, than one composed of prisoners. "You are all down on your luck," he said. "You've gone wrong with yourselves; and worst of all, you have gone wrong with God."

He then told of a desperate crook, who had spent forty years in crime, and who, when he got out of jail for the last time, was sixty years old. An old associate met him at the door and took him to the Army, and for the next seventeen years he was an active worker in their ranks. When the transformed criminal died thousands attended his funeral. The General then pleaded with his hearers to confess their sins, and in that way get right with God.

It was while he was on this tour that the Founder was introduced to a number of government correctional officials. Reporting on a conversation with the Attorney General, Mr. Colin Campbell, the General states: "They are building a new prison, and want us to take control of the prisoners, which may prove a new and important departure. Mr. Campbell studied law in the offices of our solicitors in Toronto, and therefore knows something about us." We don't hear of anything materializing from this proposal.

While in Winnipeg, General Booth had an interview with Chief Judge Howell, of Manitoba. Here is the General's report: "The Judge wound up by recommending that we should acquire the Island of St. Helena, and receive criminals from all English speaking parts of the world, see that they did not get away, and leave them to govern themselves. I replied that the first part of the suggestion was alright, and carefully thought out, but as to their governing themselves, I thought it would be an impossibility. 'Well,' said he, 'let The Salvation Army manage them, that is more like it.' And he promised to give us every co-operation." Nothing apparently developed from this proposal either.

The first Juvenile Court in Canada came into existence in Winnipeg on February 5, 1909. The interesting fact is that it was held in a Juvenile Detention Home operated by the Army in that city. Staff-Captain and Mrs. McAmmond were in charge of the home and set up the courtroom in the living room of the home.

Back in London in that same year the Founder paid a visit to Horfield Prison, near Bristol. This is how he describes the event: "My taxi took me inside the court of the prison, where I was received by the Governor and some other officials, and preceded by a couple of Curates. The Chaplain being absent, we proceeded into the Prison Chapel. The audience--men and women--formed, as is usual in such gatherings, a wretched spectacle; specially was it so with the women--poor things; they appeared to my imperfect vision a desolation of desolations. I must confess that I felt more than a little constrained and awkward as I faced my audience, and this was somewhat increased as I went on.

"I gave out two verses of the old song 'There is a fountain,' and instead of praying myself, I asked Commissioner Railton. Lawley sang, with delightful influence, his song 'Give them a Welcome' and I talked my talk. After, I got hold of my strange hearers' attention and I think their hearts. At the close I announced that if any would like to be spoken to about their souls, that I was leaving officers behind me who would be glad to see them for that purpose in their cells. Thirty-one expressed such a wish, and of this number 29 professed repentance and promised to serve God and by His help live a better life."

In reviewing his ministry, just prior to his death, the General stated, "I might have chosen to devote my life to the interests of the criminal world. The hundreds of thousands of poor wretches who are pining in the prison cells while we are sitting here at ease, ought to have our sympathy and help. We have done something for the criminal, but it is only the commencement of a mighty work the Army is destined to do for this unhappy class."

In 1917 the City of Winnipeg decided to introduce women into the Police Force. One of the first women so employed was Adjutant Andrews who had previously been Matron of the Kildonan Industrial Home. One of the Adjutant's responsibilities was to interview all the women who came into custody of the Morality Department of the police. She was frequently able to counsel these girls and to find good homes where they would come under beneficial influences.

Major Hobbins commenced serving as a volunteer probation officer in London, Ontario, in 1944 under the auspices of the Army. His work developed to the point where he was employed as a full time probation officer in 1949. Thus the Army moved into the field of probation services.

In recent years, the field of community corrections has come into much prominence and The Salvation Army has been much involved in this development. At present the department is involved in the Victim Offender Reconciliation Program, the Victim-Witness Program, the Bail Verification Program. It operates nine Community Resource Centers in Ontario. In the Province of British Columbia, The Salvation Army co-ordinates Legal Aid Services. Correctional Services officers are and continue to be, vitally interested in any avenue of service where they can assist as part of the caring community.

In the United States, Salvation Army correctional work would date its beginnings to 1885 when the first Prison-Gate Home in that country became operative. Since then,

118

the work has progressed and now extends to all parts of the country. Many outstanding officers have made their contribution to this development among whom two in particular are noted.

One of the first to leave his mark on the pages of the history of corrections in that land was Ensign Thomas Anderson. He was instrumental in founding the Brighter Day League, an association designed to bring meaning and purpose into the prisoner's life. In time, this League spread to all parts of the United States and had branches in this country. The Ensign also formed the Lifer's Club, a unique society starting with a membership of six convicted murderers at Sing Sing. This club grew until it had an enrollment of more than 400 lifers.

When one thinks of Salvation Army correctional work in the United States, another name always comes to mind, the name of Stanley Sheppard. While still a young officer, Captain Sheppard became intensely involved in the cause of corrections. Because of his ability in this field and his concern for the inmates he was given the position and responsibility of Chief Parole Officer for the State of New York. Another and unique privilege was when he was honored by being elected to the presidency of the American Correctional Association. The Captain, in addition to his work in the correctional field, was also Deputy Bandmaster and cornet soloist of the New York Staff Band.

In Europe the earliest record of work among the prisoners is culled from a report in *The War Cry* of May 24, 1890, where we note that a sergeant and two sisters had visited the prison in Rotterdam in the Netherlands.

In the last year of his life, the Founder was conducting a spiritual campaign in Denmark. While there, he took the opportunity to speak to the prisoners in the jail in Copenhagen. Afterwards one of the prisoners spoke to the prison chaplain: "I am so glad I set that house on fire in Jyland." The chaplain, startled, queried, "Carl, Carl, what do you mean?" "Oh," said he, "If I had not done that I should never have heard the General!"

Away off in India, correctional work got an early start. In 1888 a Prison-Gate Home had been opened in Bombay. Within 18 months, 200 criminals had passed through its doors. Many of these became converts and a few were accepted as officers. A leading Gujerati newspaper, in a survey of the Army's correctional work at that time said: "We may be ever so amused and grieved at the ways of The Salvation Army in converting the natives, and we may say as much as we like against them, but upon one subject we must say words of praise for these soldiers; that is, concerning the praiseworthy endeavors which The Salvation Army is making towards the improving and making honest, and setting to work, of the poor, fallen people released from the jails.

"We have a natural aversion for thieves, rogues, drunkards and villains; but God has created them also, men like us, and in their fallen state it is our duty to do all that we can to reform them and keep them from their evil ways. This duty The Salvation Army is performing in a most honorable manner, and is giving a perfect lesson for others to follow."

On the sunny island of Bermuda, the first policewoman was a Canadian Salvation Army officer, Major Alice Uden. The island authorities were very concerned about problems related to drunkenness, poverty, immorality and the suffering of children. While the Major was on the island social legislation was put into effect for the protection of children. The Major strongly influenced the passing of this legislation that was known as "The Protection of Children Act."

That the Army is needed in correctional ministry, that there is a peculiar and particular role for us to play was clearly stated by Dr. Gilmoure, the Parole Commissioner for Ontario, back in 1918. These are the doctor's words: "The idea that prison makes men better is a fallacy. The law can punish, but it seldom reforms men. As a rule, the contaminating influences of prison life tend to make men worse, and discharged prisoners will do with impunity acts they would have scorned to do before they were imprisoned. Thus there is a great need for some moral and spiritual force within the prison walls to counteract and overcome this evil influence. That force is supplied by The Salvation Army. The religious services they conduct, and the personal and kindly contact of the Army officers with the men are of inestimable value."

IN FRENCH CONVICT SETTLEMENTS

By S. Carvosso Gauntlett

From "Social Evils the Army Has Challenged"

Published by
Salvationist Publishing and Supplies
London (1946)

The problem of the overseas penal settlements of the French Republic--with which The Salvation Army grappled in the years preceding the Second World War--is not, strictly speaking, a "social evil" like those with which this series has dealt so far. It is the outcome, however unfortunate, of an attempt to solve another problem--or rather two: the safest and most profitable disposal of convicts, and the situation in French Guiana after the abolition of slavery decreed by Parliament in Paris in 1848.

By that decree, Guiana, "the marvelous garden of Equatorial France," was deprived in one day of all its manpower. The liberated Negroes were able to live without much work, by fishing and collecting the wild fruits of the forests. The colonists were faced with total ruin. Within two years, the primeval forest had overrun the cultivated land and less than ten acres remained cultivated throughout the countryside! So convicts were to supply the required labor.

In 1852 the first convicts were sent to Guiana from France. By the end of that year no fewer than 2,200 had been landed. An average of 1,200 convicts have been sent practically every year since then to Guiana penal settlements--at Saint Laurent-du-Maroni and at Cayenne on the mainland: and on the "Isles of Salvation" as, ironically enough, they are called. These latter consist of Devil's Island (the smallest), Royal Island and St. Joseph.

But the climate and the conditions under which the men live are so terrible that, despite the importation of a total of 70,000 men, the convict population of the Settlement has long been decreasing by 400 a year!

Let us consider the different classes of men in these Settlements, or the stages at which they had arrived. The first are the *transportés*--described by Péan as

> *men found guilty by a jury and sentenced by a judge to hard labor. They may have committed murder or manslaughter; burglaries, armed thefts or ordinary thefts; or certain immoral acts. "Transportation" is to give forced labor the character of punishment and intimidation, to contribute to the condemned man's reformation, to*

safeguard society, and to further colonization by the convicts' labor.

In August 1933, when The Salvation Army arrived in French Guiana, the number of "transported" men was 3,303. Some of these men--according to their conduct and the time they have served--are allowed to secure jobs as servants in private houses; or they have been "let out"--ceded--or assigned to work for private individuals. They return to the Settlement each evening; the employer pays the authorities so much per day.

The physical condition of the convicts, as well as their spiritual state, deteriorates terribly amid the stench of immorality, in which all the vices germinate and grow. Each new arrival contributes all he has of vices, diseases, corruption and obscene stories. As Péan says,

> *the horror of Convict Land is the hell in the convict himself. Its torture is due not to the military warder, but to the convict's corrupt nature, with its terrible demands and unquenchable thirst which drive him to the vices he abhors, and in the end destroy in him all that is human.*

The Army's pioneers found also some 1,700 *relégués*--"relegated" men, who are considered incurable and sent to the Camp at St. Jean du Maroni--and about twenty *déportés*, "deported" political prisoners guilty of high treason or who have escaped the death penalty. These live in isolation on Devil's Island proper, need not work, can correspond freely, and after five years' good conduct may secure permission to live at Cayenne, where some of them engage in trades.

Those in whom The Salvation Army was particularly interested were the *libérés*, "liberated" men: over 1,500 in 1933. Criminals condemned to less than eight years penal servitude must, after serving their sentence, remain in Guiana for a further number of years equal to the term of their sentence--hence the name of *doublage*. The "Administration" no longer houses or feeds them; in fact, is not interested in them--except to try to capture and then punish them if they attempt to escape across the frontiers of French Guiana. The intention behind this law of *doublage* was to prevent the return of convicts to France (the high cost of the return voyage is another deterrent) and to assure the Colony a constant supply of manpower.

The plight of the *libérés* is the most pitiable of all. They leave the Convict Settlement enfeebled, morally corrupted and brutalized. On account of their vices, nobody is willing to employ them. Most of them become drunken idlers--beggars or thieves--despised by the civil population.

About twenty years ago public opinion in France began to demand some amelioration of conditions in the Penal Settlements.

At the beginning of the century (says Major Péan in *Devil's Island*) *a perturbing report was published by Pastor Richard; then came letters from the convicts that had escaped the censorship of the Penitentiary Administration and further revealed the reprehensible state of affairs. A tragic book was written on the subject by the anarchist, Liard-Courtois, who lived in the Penal Settlement for five years. This was followed by a series of articles by various journalists, notably those written by Jacques Dur, and culminated in 1925 with the alarum sounded by Albert Londres in his contributions to the* Petit Parisien. *His book,* Au Bagne, *which followed, at last thoroughly awakened public opinion.*

Government decrees issued toward the end of that year--1925--"designed to improve the conditions of the convicts, reduce the authority of the warders, and decrease and regulate disciplinary measures," did not achieve much. Three years later, The Salvation Army secured Government permission to send an officer to Guiana for the purpose of a first-hand investigation and exploration of the possibility of some work of amelioration on behalf of the convicts and liberated men.

In July 1928, Charles Péan was dispatched to the Penal Settlements. Two years later appeared one of the most tragic and terrible books in Salvation Army literature--*Terre de Bagne* (Convict Land). It contained Péan's journal from July 17 to September 13, 1928, including a month's close inspection of the Guiana Settlements.

Péan received a cordial welcome from the authorities in Guiana, as well as from many of the convicts and *libérés*. One of the remarkable features in his record is the attitude of the men in charge of the Settlement and of the Governor of Guiana. The latter expressed to the Salvationist investigator the hope that the Army would not only seek to undertake ameliorative efforts, but succeed in abolishing the *doublage* residence. The Governor's final word was: "I beg of you to use all your influence to have the Penal Settlement suppressed altogether."

Major Péan saw the various sections of Convict Land in all their stark horror. One of the worst experiences was a visit to the "New Camp," which at a distance looked inviting, but soon revealed itself as the "ante-room of the grave, the very door of hell." Here were housed over 260 sick and dying men, suffering from the most repugnant diseases--tuberculosis, paralysis, syphilis, cancer, leprosy. Rarely did even a doctor call. "No one who has visited the 'New Camp' can have any difficulty in imagining hell," says Péan.

Another dark picture is given of the isle of Saint-Joseph, with its black cells of solitary confinement, in which are locked away those who have tried to escape or been guilty of disciplinary or other grave delinquencies. There they spend from six months to five years of their convict existence. The madmen are also kept here, and their screams and other outbursts attract the attention of passersby.

In some ways even more terrible appears the Relegation Camp at Saint-Jean--"a rotting scrap-heap of humanity, the dead end of the Settlement." Epileptics and idiots and such like here live herded together with paralysed, tubercular, syphilitic and cancerous men--all in nameless misery.

But worst of all, to Péan, was the prevailing hopelessness.

A man sentenced to relegation is simply a
variety of convict, just as slime is a variety of mud

(he wrote). *What generally characterizes him is the terrifying number of convictions. He is recidivist. He has stolen often--very often--little or much.*

Arrived at the Penal Settlement, he continues to steal; it has become a passion with him. Some have ten, fifteen, twenty convictions; others have thirty or even more. Few murderers are to be found among them.

In the Relegation Camp the regimen is the same as in the other camps. What makes the situation of these convicts worse than that of the convicts of Saint-Laurent--who, nevertheless, have committed worse crimes--is that relegation is always for life! Not more than two percent obtain a pardon.

The whole question of the guilt of these men appeared as one of the great problems. Many were thoroughly bad; others had committed a capital crime in a moment of mad anger or under the influence of drink. But some few appeared to be quite innocent of the crime of which they had been accused, and a large number had committed offences or crimes which certainly did not seem to warrant condemnation to this hell on earth. A man was considered a criminal even if he had been caught in the *attempt* to commit robbery with violence--if he had so much as broken a lock in order to steal, though the robbery had not occurred. The intention was enough!

The Camp Commandant told the Salvation Army officer: "I expected to find here dangerous bandits, and I find weak types of character, mainly peaceable, but of feeble will and spirit. Some are mentally deficient pilferers, not clever enough to escape from the gendarmes, nor sufficiently intelligible to profit by their exploits."

To which Péan added:

I feel sick at the thought that these relegated men are victims rather than culprits, and that the law in hitting them has missed its proper objective. Evidently the main objective now is to get rid of these recidivists. The solution is simple, but not very worthy. It seems to me that to be condemned

*to imprisonment for life in the Penal Settlement is
a very severe punishment for men who are habitual
thieves. If relegation freed the country from those
wholesale defrauders who fleece honest people of
their savings, something might be said for it. But
that kind is usually much too clever to be caught.
Relegation is reserved for those who know neither
how to live well or how to steal successfully!*

Quite a few of the men in the Settlement had had
some contact with *l'Armée du Salut* in France. The Army
wanted, of course, to help them all, though the
investigator's chief interest was centered in the more than
two thousand *libérés*--about half of whom roamed in the
bush, where many perished without anyone worrying about
them.

The really critical period of a convict's life begins after
he has served his sentence and begins his *doublage*.
Deprived of food and lodging, and shut *out* of prison, only
a few find occasional occupation, and then only if they are
skilled mechanics, masons or painters, etc. The others just
earn a few odd coppers when they can, spending them on
tafia, cheap raw rum, with fifty per cent alcohol content.
Under the influence of this vile liquor, normally decent
men became raving and vicious. Such an idle existence
soon makes the men hate themselves; they become
disgusted with life, live by plunder or similar expedients,
sleep anywhere and eat little and rarely. They become
like some evil flotsam, carried along and buffeted without
resisting. They have nothing more to lose, and are ready
for anything. Some become so dejected by this terrible law
of *doublage* that they do all they can to be condemned
once more to the Convict Settlement.

In Europe (wrote Major Péan) *internment in
the Convict Settlement is imagined to be an
inhuman punishment simply because of the
scandalous treatment meted out to the men.
Actually it is made odious chiefly by the degrading
vices which prevail, by the absence of obligatory
work, the lack of right ideas of punishment, the
absence of all justice; by the sufferings engendered
by liberating a man after subjecting him to a
system which forces him to become physically,
mentally and morally lower than he was when he*

*arrived at the Settlement--and then condemning
him to living conditions worse than those of his
imprisonment!*

*It seems impossible that in this twentieth
century such an altogether scandalous and futile
system could exist; that over four hundred warders,
employees, deputy directors and directors should be
engaged in a penal service, the only result of which
is the almost complete physical and moral
degradation of 6,000 men, at a cost of thirty
million francs a year.*

Of the few *libérés* able to obtain work, hardly any
manage to save enough to pay for the long voyage home
to France. One man, after several years in the Convict
Settlement, had his case revised and was found innocent.
He was given a small indemnity, but this did not even
cover his fare to France. And though he had been proved
not guilty, he was still looked upon as a convict.

The thought of wives, mothers and other loved ones
tortured many of the men in the Guiana Settlements.
Péan wrote of one who, for a not very serious crime, had
spent ten years on the rock made famous by Dreyfus. He
had just obtained his pardon, and was earning 250 francs
per month at a job he had obtained. By eating only one
meal a day, he hoped to obtain decent clothes and save up
the large sum of 2,000 francs for the return voyage. All
the time he was thinking of his unhappy old mother living
in France in utter misery. Tears filled his eyes when he
spoke of her.

Could the Army help him to find work when he
returned to France, he asked the Major. His one thought
was to be of some assistance to his mother and to make
up for all the distress he had caused her.

If a man really managed to get back to France, who
would employ him--his only reference being from Convict
Land.

In the summer of 1933--five years after his first voyage
of investigation--Major Péan returned to French Guiana,
with three other Salvation Army officers, including a
married couple. Another young officer, expert in

agriculture, followed some time later, when the Cayenne "Farm Colony" was being opened.

Hundreds of miserable men welcomed the Salvationists. The authorities also received them kindly and endeavored to give all assistance possible. Nevertheless, the beginning of Salvation Army work in the Penal Settlement was not altogether encouraging.

A number of *libérés* clamored for employment when a huge one-story building was taken over at Saint-Laurent and fitted up as the Army's *foyer* (Home)--with dormitories, dining hall, kitchen and a hall for meetings and recreation. But on the day of the opening--when many leading men attended--the newly-engaged cook celebrated by getting drunk and being locked up. The two "house-boys" also "celebrated;" one was found under the stairs, the other in the bread trough!

Many of the Army's first "customers" indulged freely in *tafia*. By ten p.m., half of them, no longer able to find the door to the home, kept walking round the garden fence! On the morning after the opening, the officers found that the cords of the flags, half the tools from the workshop, three sacks of charcoal and all the cutlery from the restaurant had been stolen; likewise the reserve of meat and the cook's cap.

That was only the beginning. Worse was to follow, including an exceptionally tall Arab's murderous attacks on the Salvation Army Lieutenant. The first time, the officer's jaw was broken; the second, he narrowly escaped having his stomach slit open by the Arab's dagger.

The work itself was increasingly heavy. The officers' average day was from 5 a.m. to 11 p.m.--in such a climate! Yet, when the distance of their quarters from the *foyer* caused some difficulty, the Captain and his wife moved cheerfully into the home, sharing the life of these *libérés*, eating with them and sleeping under the same roof.

Rarely can any Salvationists have labored amid such degraded characters, men who had long since despaired of themselves and whose mental and nervous condition was bound to be affected by the climate. Yet this "work of amelioration" produced its converts, whose stories must be among the most remarkable to which the Army can point.

As a rule the camps were visited on Sundays. Into the "library"--an innovation since Péan's previous visit--would swarm several hundred convicts sitting, standing and even hanging from the window bars! A gramophone reproduced moving songs of salvation; the words and melody of these were soon picked up by the men, who listened most attentively to the gospel message.

For the liberated men, the officers held meetings at the *foyer*, and every Tuesday evening the Captain gathered the little group of converts for Bible study and prayer. The changed lives of such men bore magnificent testimony among the *libérés* to the power of God's grace.

The employer of one told Major Péan that before his conversion this man had been continually drunk and incapable of work. Now he no longer touched alcohol, and was a model employee. When the employer--the mayor of the town--entertained officials and numerous bottles of champagne were opened, converted *libérés* were requisitioned; the mayor knew that they would not touch a drop of the champagne! Lemonade was provided for their use.

Another convert, who had been a persistent *tafia* drinker, was appointed "guardian" of the town square. On Sundays he filled his haversack with Gospels, New Testaments and Bibles, and hawked them in the surrounding villages. When the steamer from France arrived, he would go on board and offer Bibles and Salvation Army periodicals to the passengers. Thanks to his zeal, all the crew of the steamer possess Bibles. Such success compensated the Army officers for many hardships, dangers and disappointments.

At Cayenne a big shed at the quayside was rented, to be turned into a carpenter's shop.

Later, a building with three large halls was made into a Home, called *La Maison de France* (the House of France). *Libérés* could sleep in the shelter, and in the restaurant eat their meals. A much-frequented rest-room has table games and so on.

The first meeting in the hall in this building witnessed the marriage of a young officer with a plucky girl Lieutenant who had arrived from France that morning. In *Devil's Island*, Major Péan gave a moving picture of a meeting, with the songs and testimonies of twice "liberated" men.

At the penitent form of the meeting hall not a few "hopeless" men have found life in Christ. One, unable to work or even to walk about, sat himself outside a shop and distributed Gospels to passersby. In less than a fortnight 800 accepted these booklets and he sold eight New Testaments and fifteen complete Bibles.

The Cayenne officers also visited the penitentiary and the hospital, where they conduct meetings and distribute copies of *En Avant (The War Cry)* and other good literature. From time to time they also pay visits to the three "Isles of Salvation."

In some ways the most interesting of the Army's ventures in French Guiana has been the Farm Colony at Montjoly, eight miles from Cayenne. A peninsula--facing toward the far-distant France--was purchased and, aided by *libérés,* the officers cleared away the jungle growth, irrigated the land, and developed a market garden and a banana plantation, a chicken farm, piggery, etc. They also erected buildings, which they furnished with tables, chairs, beds, etc., made at the Army's workshop in Cayenne.

Here, too, meetings have been held and conversions registered. The latter, one senses, have been due particularly to the personal influence of the officers, who share the men's hard life and labor and receive as salary hardly more than they.

Major Péan records a brief conversation with a *libéré* whom he hardly recognized from a previous encounter, so changed was he.

"In a year I shall soon be through, you know," continues the lamplighter.

"And what will you do then?"

131

"Oh, there is no question about that. I shall have earned my passage. Vive la France! And long live The Salvation Army, for without you I should have croaked in some hole."

The Lieutenant joined us (said Péan), *for night had fallen and he was afraid that I should break my neck on my return journey to the farm.... On leaving the kitchen-garden I remarked to the Lieutenant:*

"This man is a relégué, sentenced eighteen times for theft--and you make a watchman of him!"

The Lieutenant smiled.

"He is the only one who does the rounds conscientiously," he said. "You see he was converted several months ago, and now gives full satisfaction."

At the time of Major Péan's second visit, of which he wrote in *Le Salut des Parias* (The Salvation of the Pariahs), the men working at Montjoly received--in addition to board, lodging and pocket money--the equivalent of forty francs per month. They were encouraged to save this, and when 800 francs had been accumulated the Army would give in exchange a ticket for France costing 1,700 francs.

Back to France! The Army has enabled hundreds of men to return to their native land--men who had not believed that they would ever see it again.

The returning men were up against great difficulties. Their impaired health, their police record and the suspicion of the public were formidable enough. Apart from those who have been received back into their families or into The Salvation Army's social institutions, very few have survived the ordeal.

Devil's Island gives a memorable description of the arrival back in France--or, in several instances, in North Africa--of such men, of some after thirty or more years' absence. One moving story concerns a young man whose return the Army was able to expedite in view of the serious illness of his mother.

> *The father waits at the railway station of Saint-Lazare in Paris* (wrote Major Péan). *Since yesterday afternoon he has been telephoning us constantly to know whether the mailboat has arrived, and now, as he paces the platform, he cannot restrain his impatience. From the last third class coach descend a group of men; their suitcases, deck-chairs, torn and shabby clothes, and the tan of their skin make doubt impossible. Surely these are our Salvation Army party from Guiana.*

> *"Is Verber there?" I inquire of the group.*

> *A young man turns, "I am Verber."*

> *The two men embrace amid tears.*

> *"How is mother?" murmurs the son.*

> *"You must come quickly!" is the only reply.*

> *When father and son reach home, the dying woman has strength left only to put her emaciated hand on the head of the son as he kneels at her bedside. It is her last movement. While the prodigal sobs: "Forgive me, mother, oh, forgive me!" she passes away, content at last to have looked once more on the face of her boy.*

Everywhere, *l'Armée du Salut* has been in evidence as the Army of the Helping Hand. What magnificent work these French Salvationists have done!

Besides its ameliorative work in Guiana, the Army in France for years worked hard to secure the *abolition* of the Penal Settlement--an endeavor which, as we have seen, had the support of the authorities out there.

The ways of governments are often devious and difficult to understand. After a suspension of convict transports, another "shipment" was sent to Guiana toward the end of 1938--to the bitter disappointment of the reformers, among whom Salvationists were very prominent.

Ironically, men condemned for major crimes were to serve their sentences in French prisons specially adapted for this purpose; but men condemned to relegations or exile in consequence of numerous but generally *minor* delinquencies were still to be sent to Guiana.

However, that chapter in the tragic story was a short one. The war--which incidentally cut off the handful of officers in Guiana from moral and financial support by their comrades in France--made further transportation of convicts impossible. The latest word is that the new French Government not only will discontinue the practice but will, as soon as feasible, bring back to France the men still in Convict Land.

The Army's work in that terrible field, already curtailed by the abnormal decreases in the convict population, which has had no reinforcements for five years, will thus soon come to an end. But The Salvation Army will never forget the heroic labors, under most distressing conditions, of the French officers out there. It glories also in the remarkable success that has crowned the persistent and self-sacrificing challenge to the system on the part of its comrades in France.

In October 1952, the last of the convicts returned to their native land. "The *Bagne* has lasted a century. Now it is nothing but a story."

V. War

In his introduction, Booth commends the process by which national "disputes are to be settled by arbitration," rather than by war, about which he declares, "Of all the Hell-making scourges ever contrived by Satan, that ever flourished among the nations of the earth, war seems to be not only the bloodiest, but the silliest."

But his vision is wider--a war which is productive of "more miseries than that by which nations settled their differences in open combat." This war he calls "Fighting of Every Description."

"The spirit of this war," he declares, "rends the unity of families, makes husbands fight their wives, and children kick at the rule and control of their parents. It even makes the children hate and curse and tear each other. This warfare has been the parent of almost every gory murder.

"This spirit is responsible for all the family feuds, and wrongdoing, and nagging, which make life one long bitterness to such multitudes of people."

The answer is found in the Prince of Peace. He concludes, "If he is involved in some bitter quarrel, salvation will lead him to make peace with his enemies."

DISARMAMENT

By Evangeline Booth

Excerpted from "The Staff Review"

Published by
The Salvation Army
International Headquarters
London (January 1931)

I want to speak to you of the merciful and intelligent endeavors to promote disarmament. No organization anywhere at work in the world is in closer contact than The Salvation Army with the meaning of war, and, indeed, of all the material disasters which from time to time spread ruin among the people. If there be fire, if there be flood, if there be accident, if there be sudden death, it is the Army that, in countless instances, is first upon the scene of disasters to aid sufferers. It is no matter for surprise, then, that with acute anxiety we have been watching the developments of the Disarmament Conference in London, consisting of the five leading naval powers of the world! We support all measures by which disarmament is promoted by international diplomacy, so relieving common people of the heavy burden of taxation, so minimizing the risks of a further calamitous conflict, so preparing the way for permanent peace among all nations.

In operation and spirit, The Salvation Army is international. It is inseparably and vitally linked up with the highest interests of the human family, and there is, perhaps, no other evangelical organization which by its international structure, has invested its future so whole-heartedly in the effort to promote goodwill among all peoples.

While all the measures for peace for which we had hoped and still continue to hope have not been accomplished as yet, the world is moving forward and upward towards the great reconciliation. The brutal barbarity that destroys life and property is yielding to common sense, and will assuredly be buried deeper and deeper, under an accumulating consideration of man for his fellowman. "Peace on earth" will be more than a glorious carol from the skies. It will be the practical policy of reasonable statesmanship.

My comrades, I believe the time is fast approaching when war will be regarded by all men of religion, learning, and thought as a stalking monster of barbaric irrationalism. The principle of the stronger striking down the weaker to settle international disagreements, or even as compensation for international wrongs, is bound to surrender to the greater principles of universal justice, and these have no sure foundation but in the religion of Jesus Christ.

137

Peace is not merely a negative cessation of bloodshed and hatred. It is an opportunity for positive and constructive spiritual and social service and sacrifice. Why do we, as a Salvation Army, desire that the world cease from fighting *against* flesh and blood? It is because we desire the more eagerly to promote the fight *for* flesh and blood. We hate to destroy people because we yearn to help people; and when the good of all peoples shall be all men's rule, then and only then will universal peace, between religions, races, and sovereignties, fling its mantle across the shoulders of the world and, as an abiding shaft of light, illuminate the homes of countless millions with the Sun of Righteousness, rising with healing in His wings.

DOAN QUAN CUU THE

(The Salvation Army)

By Barbara A. Exline

From "Beyond the Battlefield"

Published by
The Salvation Army
USA Eastern Territory
New York (1985)

Mrs. Xuan was a mother of ten and with her husband and family lived in a refugee camp in one nine-by-ten-foot room. Her husband had been mentally ill for ten years and was of little use to the family for support or guidance; hence, Mrs. Xuan made cakes to sell at the market. From this, the family managed to obtain the equivalent of $1.25 daily to support its 12 members.

Mrs. Xuan's first contact with the Salvation Army team was through our medical services as she had come to our clinic. Our doctor immediately referred her to surgery because of a tumor in her left breast. The tumor was found to be malignant, and a radical mastectomy was performed. After post-operative care, Mrs. Xuan developed metastasis, and the eventual prognosis was "terminal."

As a result, the family would be left without any means of support. Our social worker picked up where our medical team phased out and made frequent visits to the home, bringing food and medicine. Through the encouragement of our social welfare staff, Mrs. Xuan's oldest daughter took over cooking of the cakes to sell on the market and cared for the younger members of the family. Another daughter was supplied with material to make saleable items. The children were then introduced to Salvation Army youth services, which provided them with schooling and recreational activities.

All of this service gave Mrs. Xuan the emotional support and courage to face the future. Before her death, she was able to see that her family had a chance for survival.

In essence, this was how Salvation Army medical, social welfare, and youth services functioned in South Vietnam, where "The Salvation Army" became translated as *Doan Quan Cuu The*. Our success in that country lay in the multiplicity of services we were able to provide.

Naturally all individual cases did not have, nor did they need, the interrelated association of all our services, but the fact that we succeeded was because a person's need could be communicated to us regardless of which branch of our services the individual first encountered.

Each morning after breakfast our teams would pack up their cardboard boxes of supplies and carry them to our vehicles. Then we would be off to our designated areas. The need for our services carried us to many locations in Saigon and its outskirts. Some of the seven refugee camps we went to were small, with a population of 2,000; the largest housed about 20,000 refugees.

It was necessary to stop at checkpoints (bunkers manned by the military) along our way since the previous night's events may have made it dangerous to travel further. In some camps, even when the military had searched every home for infiltrators, security deteriorated so fast that we could visit only in the morning.

Saigon had been called "the Paris of the Orient" because of the French influence on its streets and buildings. The formerly picturesque city had been bordered by gorgeous flowers and noted for its charming and beautiful people. Can Ranh Bay and Vung Tau had been popular with their miles of white sandy beaches, and Da Lat had been another famous resort area. The historic "Imperial City" of Hue had once fascinated travelers with its artifacts and elegance.

Before the war, many Vietnamese had been successful farmers and businessmen and owned impressive villas. But war had taken its toll and was no respecter of persons or their backgrounds. Many had given up their rubber plantations and sugar-cane crops in exchange for their lives. Cinnamon orchards, machinery, and businesses of all kinds had been left at a standstill as the population fled from invaders. In Saigon itself, colorful shops and lucrative business establishments had been bombed; their owners had been left with nothing except a few cracked dishes and the clothes they were wearing.

Homes had been destroyed, burned, and leveled by rockets and artillery fire as the Communists used the personal property of the Vietnamese as main entry routes during their invasion attempts. The destruction they had left in their wake was appalling, as though someone had pounded away at your heart with a sledgehammer! The people were poor, having suffered tremendous losses at the hand of the invader. Now many were at refugee camps, terrorized by war, living in a regressive state compared with their former lifestyles, and none of it was by choice.

As we attempted to drive through the narrow, muddy, and rutted roads of Saigon, we saw the depth of disaster, the pinnacle of poverty, and the factuality of fear that hovered over the area like an unpredictable cloud.

The refugee camps were the actual homes of the war victims, but to call them "home" would be an overstatement. Housing conditions were inadequate, sanitary conditions gave extreme cause for alarm, social conditions were pathetic, and essential basics were all deficient.

Each family, having from two to 15 members, was given a nine-by-ten-foot room. The muddy ground constituted the flooring, and the walls were nothing more than bare wooden slats held together by rusted nails. Yet here the refugees would cook their meals on an open fire, eat, and keep all their belongings, even a bicycle if they were fortunate enough to have one. In the evenings they would stretch out a few hammocks and throw mats on the ground until the room was transformed into a king-sized bunk bed. Very few camps had any form of electricity, and those that did provided only one light bulb per room that could be turned on from nine to eleven p.m. only.

As we walked through these camps, we found the penetrating smells and sights deplorable. Past every door flowed a scum-covered stream filled with muck and garbage. Although each camp had an outside community toilet, many found it to be too long a walk and added their waste closer to home, intensifying the already repellent smell. We saw children playing in the same stinking conglomeration--their only form of fun.

One refugee camp we serviced was erected on what had once been the city garbage dump. The strong smell told its ancestry. Where the camp ended, the garbage dump still continued and served as a playground for camp inhabitants. In this canyon of pauperage, some adults would be seen scrounging around in hopes of finding something to salvage.

Each family received a ration of rice from the Vietnamese government, and that was their basic diet. Fortunately, there is something about rice that doesn't make it distasteful three times a day, but I'm sure they would have preferred other foods added to it. For most of them, rice was about all they had except on occasion when they would splurge and purchase some fish or vegetables. Per capita, per young person, their average consumption of meat *annually* would probably have amounted to one "Big Boy" hamburger.

In loving these dear folks so much, wanting to be totally devoted to them, I felt pangs of remorse as I was daily brought face-to-face with the reality of how they all had to live, cramped together in such poor conditions.

Never let it be said, however, that these people were lazy or uninterested in bettering themselves. I was constantly impressed with their ambition and initiative. In the face of adverse conditions, they exemplified more fortitude and skill than I could ever hope to gain. Imagine their small, dingy rooms being the place of productivity during the day! It was phenomenal! In visiting one of the girl's homes, I discovered that her father, sitting on a stool with only a sharp knife and hammer as his tools, was fashioning the most beautiful patent-leather shoes--custom made originals. After class, two of my girls would hurry home and with only a solid square peg and a bolt of wire, they would manufacture bobby pins. Others with paper, paste, and cardboard created attractive paper bags and boxes for various businesses. Every home had some new trade to entice your curiosity, from efficient tailoring to hand grinding of eyeglass lenses. Many sold their items in private mini-markets in the camps: others traveled to the "big time" in Saigon.

In years to come, these industrious refugees would undoubtedly lift themselves above their deplorable circumstances, but at that time, they needed Salvation Army services, and that is why we were there.

Medical Services

Those who knew of The Salvation Army's work in Vietnam agreed that our medical personnel were instrumental in restoring health to many lives. Certainly that team endured the heaviest load of responsibility. From the outset of our work, I saw the heartbeat of this team in action when I would watch Major Eva Cosby, Dr. Li Sin Wah, and Envoy Chu Suet King pile their dilapidated boxes containing a limited supply of medicines into a car and head towards the war-torn area to bring medical relief to those who had been freshly stricken by the Tet Offensive in early 1968. The team went out even during the period of alert when everyone was ordered off the streets because of potential attacks.

At first, the youth activities--my major responsibility--were held only in the afternoon; hence, I was assigned duty with the medical team in the mornings, and it was a golden experience to work alongside this group of efficiency experts.

At an accelerated pace, we would unload our vehicle and bring everything into one of the nine-by-twelve-foot rooms assigned as a clinic. Next on the agenda was the opening ritual: the spray-gun brigade would saturate the premises, including a few mosquitoes, with insecticide. This was followed by wiping off the work areas: tables, benches, etc. Then we'd set up the medicines and put out the bandages.

Every inch of this makeshift clinic was utilized: the "waiting room" area with a few, but never sufficient, benches; the "registration" corner with files and personal-related medical data; a corner where an aide would take the temperature of each patient and make note of it on a card; the doctors' examination area; a dressing/injection area that for want of space would protrude somewhat halfway out the door; and a prescription table, which was all we could provide for the pharmacy.

My indoctrination was swift, and I quickly realized the need for medical services. It was only my second day on medical duty when Dr. Li Sin Wah asked me to go with her across the lane where she had been requested to look at a sick baby. The little girl was just three years old, and her pale color and clammy skin substantiated the fact that she had been quite ill for some time. The mother's face was sad, and drawn from sleepless nights. Her eyes were swollen from tears, and her voice quivered as she told Dr. Li that she had no way and no money to bring her baby to the hospital in Saigon. The doctor's diagnosis was dehydration. She worked with the little one, but her attempts were futile. Within a few short moments, the little body ceased to move at all; she was dead. If only we had known sooner!

The heavy turnout of new patients and repeaters signified, certainly, that the Vietnamese placed tremendous confidence in our doctors and clinic. We treated everything from colds to cancer, from minor lacerations to gun wounds. Many of the cases diagnosed were dermatitis, respiratory infections, anemia, diarrhea, skin rashes, and vitamin deficiencies stemming from inadequate food as well as filth, dirt, and exhaust fumes.

The clinic had its share of war casualties, like the lady who came with half her face blown off as a result of the bombing. War victims had sometimes been treated with traditional home-concocted remedies, tried on them by a loving parent before they even reached our clinic. Those cases were the most difficult to treat. One was a boy, who, while playing with his friends, had given way to his normal 12-year-old's curiosity and picked up an object that turned out to be a bomb. It exploded in his right hand, blowing off the thumb and the first joints of three fingers as well as badly mutilating the remaining hand. Unfortunately, his parents had tried their own remedies, and by the time the little fellow was transported to our doctor, his hand was extremely infected and irritated. Providentially, Dr. Wiese from an organization called Children Medical Relief was with us that day; immediately after examining the boy, Dr. Wiese took him to the CMR Center Hospital, where he operated on the hand and started plastic surgery the following day.

There were some fantastic voluntary agencies in Vietnam, and we all worked with one another. Many of our critical patients who needed surgery--plastic or otherwise--were sent to the CMR Center, where doctors with the finest skills labored over countless patients.

A famous plastic surgeon had sent an appeal to colleagues all over the world to donate some time to plastic surgery needs in Vietnam. International Headquarters of The Salvation Army allowed Colonel (Dr.)

Harry Williams, a plastic surgeon and British Salvation Army officer on missionary service in India, to assist for three months in the Barsky Unit of the CMR Center Hospital, Saigon. As chief medical officer at one of the largest overseas hospitals in India, Colonel Williams had developed a number of new operations for leprosy patients. In Saigon he operated in various hospitals throughout the city. He also went to refugee camps with our medical team and successfully attended to some remarkable cases. In one particular case, a rocket had hit a home, killing the parents and all the children except for a brother and sister, who were badly mutilated. The boy was seriously burned and had an arm and leg missing. His older sister, age 13, was in far worse condition. Half her face, one eye, and her nose had been completely blown off, and severe damage had been done to the remaining part of her body. I wondered how they could possibly have survived. Colonel Williams created a new girl and boy through the medium of plastic surgery, giving them a better chance at life. This was just one case out of hundreds in which his skill had inestimable results.

Having Colonel Williams to dinner was like having one of the family, but watching him at work was something else. He was so outstanding, so high on the ladder of expertise, that you would feel you had to stand on the tip of your toes to touch the bottoms of his feet.

Not all casualties had physical wounds; some victims were just unattached, unloved as a result of war, and some of these people also came to the Salvation Army team for attention. One dear lady, 80 years old, was first in line each time the clinic was in her area. She had no home, no family, no income. She wore on her back all her possessions. Her only means for keeping alive seemed to be her habitual visits to the garbage piles, where she would pick out junk to sell. This elderly soul was Major Cosby's personal concern, and you can be sure, her need for love and attention was met, along with some material needs. Like the legendary Evangeline Booth, who showed immense compassion for those in need, Major Cosby would always give the old woman her concerned attention and a sack full of clothes, rice, and other supplies.

In the early 1960s, the average lifespan of the Vietnamese was only 35 years, mainly because of intestinal infection, tuberculosis, bubonic plague, and malaria. Hence, it was not enough for the clinic to simply furnish dressings and pills. Mrs. Collins developed a preventive medicine outreach program involving immunizations. In one month alone, over and above the daily clinic administrations, a total of 4,623 inoculations were given, as follows: plague, 885; cholera, 833; smallpox, 436; polio, 1,351; and D.P.T. (diphtheria, pertussis, and tetanus in a combination shot), 1,158.

Thanks to a donation of fabric from Colonel John Baggs and officers of the Massachusetts Division, Maureen Fawcett was able to outfit her clinic aides in smart candy-striper uniforms.

That was just the beginning! Prenatal classes were added next. Later, in conjunction with our school program, our medical team came to school and distributed toothbrushes, toothpaste, soap, and washcloths and instructed the students in personal hygiene.

The climax of the extra-curricular activities of our medical staff was, I believe, the well-baby clinic. This was quite a new idea to Vietnamese mothers, but they unmistakably responded. They really loved coming each week and weighing in their babies, comparing theirs with others, etc. Proper immunizations were given to the infants as well as instructions to mothers on personal hygiene and sanitation.

Although our staff worked arduously to conquer immediate illness--to heal wounds and ease pain--we felt that education in health and sanitation was equally vital, and the team worked closely with the Vietnamese government to fill that need.

Youth Services

My main responsibility was in the youth services provided by The Salvation Army. While it all started with only a half-day of classes in one room with 60 children and a staff of two (translator and myself), our diligence was rewarded. After three years, we saw many plans and dreams come to fruition with seven schools going full force, eight hours daily, with more than 900 children and a teaching staff of 21.

The youth team was structured with a two-fold purpose: to establish varied youth activities at the refugee camps and to instruct counterpart Vietnamese school administrators and teachers in educational principles and techniques. At that time a Vietnamese citizen could be classified as a "teacher" after extending studies only three months beyond high school level. This left us a lot of opportunity to give additional instruction. I was responsible for giving training to Loan, who was considered my counterpart as school administrator. Ultimately we hoped she would be able to administer the established program when I left. Loan turned out to be a true and precious friend and most helpful in explaining Vietnamese ways.

Unfortunately, the Viet Cong resented any form of non-Communist education being pursued, and they made teachers and school children targets for their hostilities. Often the VC would stop a group of children going to school and forbid them to attend. If after the warning they continued, the VC would make an example of one of the students by ramming a bamboo shoot down his ear, breaking the child's eardrum.

I won't elaborate on what they did to teachers, but from results I'd seen, the teachers had gone through indescribable torture. Their bodies had been mangled to the extent that even a mother wouldn't recognize her own; by the time the VC had finished with their prey, no distinction could be made as to whether the bodies were male or female.

Eagerness of the Vietnamese to learn, however, made them overlook any deterrent. The children would arrive long before school opened, and if allowed, would have stayed all night. Equally sharing the desire were the teachers, who had a perpetual passion to help their young people get an education, at any risk.

Magnetic bundles of love is the only way to describe our students. They were so responsive to affection, as well as education, that you just wanted to take about 100 of them home with you each night. Yet even with your sheer delight in these young people, you had to be cautious; unfortunately, some of them had been indoctrinated to do what the VC wanted.

The publicized VC philosophy included the training of youth. They would take seven- and eight-year-old children and teach them the almanac of war, then infiltrate them back into the South.

A U.S. Army captain once asked me, "Barbara, what would you do if a six-year-old came up to your jeep with a live grenade?" His solution was to shoot the little boy in self-defense. It seems unbelievable, yet to be ignorant of the danger could be fatal.

Some military men couldn't accept the idea that little kids could be anything but "fun-loving." One U.S. troop was out doing some investigating in a village, and the sergeant would always take some ration candy and pass it out to the kids. A lieutenant warned the sergeant to watch those kids, but he never heeded. As the sergeant sat on the ground in a circle with the kids, a little fellow rolled a grenade between the sergeant's legs, killing him and others in the group.

Although Vietnam was no Sunday school picnic and we visitors to the country were under strain from fear and precautions, we really weren't reluctant or repressed when it came to pouring out our love to those kids who did need it.

The lifeblood of the Salvation Army youth program was education. In this capacity, we worked with the Vietnamese Ministry of Education. Our curriculum included science, math, Vietnamese language, history, and geography, with a few additions of music, arts and crafts, and English.

In the more affluent areas, it was customary for children attending school to wear white shirts with emblems of their school on them. Our kids were lucky if they had a shirt to wear! Generosity bridged the gap, however, when a group of people from the Salvation Army Pioneer Corps thousands of miles away in Philadelphia, Pennsylvania, sent bolt upon bolt of white material, from which we made each student a personalized shirt. A red Salvation Army shield on the pocket made a brilliant emblem, and how gorgeous the students all looked as they came to class the first day!

149

To see the pupils sitting on the floor at school wasn't an unusual sight at first. Actually we often had no choice; we felt quite fortunate to have a room with a roof! Eventually we progressed to benches, then to desks (or a facsimile thereof), a kindness of the chief and men of the camp who made those desks on their own. One school even had a light bulb; that *really* was an accomplishment!

The children became a very real part of my life as I was constantly caught up with the excitement and curiosity of uncovering each individual personality. They were consistent in their attendance, and when they were absent, they were missed and we were concerned about them. To be sure, whenever a student stayed home, it was always for a good reason. Usually it was because of illness. When one student stayed home, Dr. Li Sin Wah got word that her mother had called for the doctor and asked me to go with her to check on the child. We found the mother waiting patiently for the doctor. Her daughter Kim was only eight years old and had been unable to come to class because of third-degree burns from her waist to about two inches above her knees. A hot kerosene lamp had toppled over on her. It was so pathetic. Kim couldn't bear to straighten out her legs. As Dr. Li Sin Wah and the mother tenderly tried to cut away the home-made dressing to change it, Kim's flesh peeled off, too. Her cries pierced my heart until I thought it would bleed. I stood there and watched her beautiful face become distorted with pain, and my heart ached. With the doctor's help and medicine, Kim was soon back to class and part of a group that was most creative and exact in their work, striving for perfection, however simple the task.

Vietnamese are independent, too. I especially recall one little tyke who, when introduced to water paints, completely ignored the animals he was to color, choosing instead to change the color of the sandals he was wearing! A further illustration is an incident that took place when we were studying the word "grape." I had brought pictures of a cluster of grapes for the students to color, cut out, and paste on their baskets. One conscientious fellow, by the time I got to him, had cut each grape out individually; by the time he finished the project, his basket looked as if it had picked up a case of the German measles. Another boy decided he didn't like big purple grapes at all, and he made colored balloons out of them.

My students were so appreciative. If you gave them pencils, they acted as if you had given them the world. They would be overwhelmed with joy over a box of crayons or a writing tablet.

Earlier I told how Vietnamese find Americans unusual because of our round eyes and hair on our arms. One day a little girl in my class kept patting my long pointed nose, and she would laugh and giggle. I asked the translator what the child was saying, and he, being merciful, said, "They think you are very pretty." Of course, I knew all the time they thought my nose was a museum piece.

As I sat at my desk in the classroom one day, I had the horrifying sensation of "something" crawling up and down my legs. Looking down, I saw two children sitting under the desk touching the "film" (nylons) covering my legs. They just had to see if it was real!

The communication barrier was noticeable within the classroom, but usually we would find ourselves laughing, rather than becoming frustrated, at some of the situations it created. Many times my translator misunderstood what I wanted to say or do. One time I said to the translator, "Tell them to open their tablets and watch the board for a new word." No sooner said than done, I thought. But as I turned to write on the board, I heard the translator say *"hai ba"* (which is "two, three"), and the children all began singing a Vietnamese song--three times through!

What made such mistakes worse was that if the Vietnamese didn't understand, they never let on. Whatever you asked, it was always a nod and "yes" in reply so that you would have no way of knowing if you were understood.

One day a girl came to me and rattled out something quickly, attaching the question "yes?" She didn't have my full attention at that moment, and not really understanding what she said, I responded with a typical Vietnamese "yes" myself. The penalty for not being attentive was that I had given her my small new suitcase. That was one mistake I didn't make twice.

Language wasn't the only barrier that confronted me. Cultural differences also came into play. Loan was steeped in Vietnamese culture, and her strict upbringing caused her to adhere to all its rules. She spoke only in soft tones, never raising her voice for any reason. One day when class was extremely rowdy, I relayed a few angry words of reproof for her to translate. With my strong vocal projection, I could be heard throughout the camp, but Loan, in a way all her own, looked at me, made a circular motion around her mouth with her finger, and said, "My mouth too small!" I got the point!

Our music endeavors at school brought along with them loads of fun and climaxed in our forming a National Rhythm Band. We had every conceivable type of instrument, even a xylophone; however, some contraptions were invented on the spot, homemade out of bits of innertubes, bamboo, coconuts, sandpaper, nails, a few bottles, tin cans, and tons of imagination. Going from camp to camp really gave those instruments a short life. That's why we were so pleased when the real McCoy arrived from overseas one day. The home league of the Forbes Road Outpost, supervised by the Salvation Army corps in Greensburg, Pennsylvania, with my mother as home league secretary, had gathered rhythm band instruments and mailed them to Vietnam, where they took a real beating!

Parents of children showed a marvelous interest in their schooling and were incredibly cooperative. Placing a great value on education, they didn't just send their kids off to school; they brought them. They also watched everything we did with intense fascination.

This was exceptionally true at one camp where we opened a kindergarten. The first day parents were so eager to have their little "blessings" attend and so fearful there wouldn't be seats for them that they showed up literally at the break of dawn. For the actual enrollment, we asked if each mother would send along her child's birth certificate. I believe that every child had one! Still it took an endless amount of our time to obtain all the information. The children were very good about answering our questions, but their parents slowed the process down. We would ask a question directed to some particular child, but before he could open his mouth, his mother would shout the answer from outside the window where parents would watch the proceedings and patrol with eagle eyes. If the child didn't toe the line as Daddy expected, Daddy then barged in and took measures to remedy the situation, totally oblivious to the 35 other students and the fact that a class was in session. One father didn't agree with the way his little one had colored a picture, and when I turned around, there was Daddy perched in the midst of little babes, coloring it *his* way!

Our classes were supplemented with recreational activities twice a week that consisted of Ping-Pong, volleyball, checkers, jump rope, softball, and archery. In the last sport, the bow was bigger than the boy! Tournaments were held to develop the spirit of competition, and field days gave them opportunity to test their skills on an individual basis.

Vocational classes for the older ones were also inaugurated. The Vietnamese children showed their ability to excel in classes like hat making, carpentry, barbering, and sewing, and our total program began showing signs of a well-balanced diet.

In our desire to have the student exposed to all types of educational experience, including the cultural, we decided to add a few field trips. Going through the influential arm of U.S. Army General Creighton Abrams, we were provided by the U.S. military with transportation, via their buses. Our first stop was to the Saigon Zoo, and what a rewarding time that turned out to be!

The evening before, some of the girls helped us pop corn. And we popped ... and we popped ... and then bagged it all to be handed out to the children the following day. We also made up some petite bags of peanuts so that each child could feed the bears. The last step was making Kool-Aid and packing some cookies for all.

What a sight it was as the big bus pulled up in front of the camp! All our babes were there, dressed in their best clothes, with Daddy's oversized good hat and Mommy's best shoes. It was too precious for words. They were as excited as any child on Christmas Eve. We had made paper emblems of the Salvation Army shield, and the children pinned them proudly on their blouses and shirts. As we were stopped at the zoo gate by the guard who collected fees, he took one look at the emblems, considered us top grade, and permitted us to go through gratis.

We traveled throughout the zoo, feeding the animals, stopping at the museums, taking special interest in a Buddhist temple on the grounds, and largely ignoring the reminders of war that were strategically placed, even in the zoo.

Everyone had brought a lunch, and we ended our tour with a picnic, serving the Kool-Aid and cookies. I was really out of place with my American sandwich: fish heads and rice would have been more in style!

We looked a little different on our return trip. Hats were missing from our heads, bare feet stuck out in the aisle as some youngsters curled up, sound asleep. Others contentedly munched on their popcorn. All of them were exhausted, but it had been a memorable experience. Many of these young folk had known nothing but the ugliness of war. It was a new world for them to be able to finally take in some of life's beauty.

The zoo trip was a springboard into many more field trips, and the students were equally intrigued with the Cogido Paper Mill, a sugar company, and other points of interest.

The PTA was unheard of in Vietnam, but the titanic interest of our parents in education tempted us with ideas for such an organization. We sent letters to the parents, surveying the potential and explaining the functions of a PTA in hopes of finding at least 50 interested folk. We were overwhelmed with some 238 replies. And we still had four camps to go! For this reason, we organized into smaller PTA groups by class, and with charts, program ideas, and capable staff, we held our first orientation sessions. The response was just wonderful. Many questions were raised regarding the children's education, The Salvation Army, the future, etc. At the close of the meeting, the parents could not say enough in appreciation. It produced a warm feeling as the teachers mingled afterwards with the parents, who were most likely bragging a little about their offspring. It was another step in the right direction and resulted in teachers holding PTA conferences in *all* camps.

Graduation was another highlight for students, ending the prescribed course for the year. Alice Murdoch, another staff member in our youth program and one with a master's degree in education, is certainly due commendation for her many accomplishments in this area. She was able to get the Vietnamese Ministry of Education to affix its official seal to all the report cards and graduation certificates.

The ceremonies were ever so impressive, with many participants. Students, teachers, parents, Salvation Army personnel, and Saigon officials all played a part. They seemed extremely pleased about our schools and what had been accomplished in them.

"The proof of the pudding is in the eating," says the old proverb, and we certainly found this true regarding the Vietnamese teachers we had been training to take over. At graduation we reflected on how they had assumed leadership roles in a most magnificent way. How proud we had been to watch their development, to see such poise, and to witness such organization. We could never say our time and effort among them had been wasted.

We had deliberately scheduled time for a teachers' training program when we discovered the need for something more intensified than quick weekly meetings with teachers, or hours at the end of a day or on a Saturday night. Our impetus came from Dr. Mai Tam, a Catholic priest who was the only Vietnamese in the country with a Ph.D. in child psychiatry. He was busy teaching at universities in the cities of Saigon, Hue and Da Lat. When I occasionally invited this entertaining person to join me and a few friends for dinner, he usually turned the conversation to the subject of education and the dire need for trained Vietnamese teachers. His inspirational talks and philosophy gave birth to our Institute of Instruction.

For one year we planned for the week-long teachers' institute, concentrating on educational and vocational aspects of training. All 28 of our staff members attended and claimed it to be a most profitable time. One teacher evaluated it as "a real opening of the mind," and our evaluation of the institute was that it was all we had longed for it to be. We offered a course developed by the U.S. Agency for International Development that included topics such as "The American Effort in Vietnam," "Cross-culture Problems in Working Together," and "Vietnam, Know Your Country." All this was presented in unique fashion with drama, panel discussions, movies, and other techniques. We were most honored when Dr. Tam gave three afternoons of his time gratis for our institute. The doctor held combined group sessions on "Motivations of Behavior."

Mrs. Collins had a most impressive session on first aid in the classroom. It was evident throughout her many demonstrations that much work and thought was behind her presentations. Group participation, such as practice wrapping broken arms and putting on splints, brought to surface many hidden talents, and the teachers were able to mix their learning with a bit of fun. I did suggest, however, that some should stick to carpentry!

Loan and Diep Mi Kieu, our administrative aides, held sessions involving recreation and handicrafts. Then we branched into educational and vocational workshops. With these, too, we were able to acquire some of Vietnam's most wanted men, intellectually speaking, who served as guest lecturers.

The climax of the institute was a recognition dinner. Certificates of appreciation, signed by The Salvation Army's Commissioner Samuel Hepburn (then national commander of the Army in the United States) were presented to all instructors. Attractive diplomas, etched in Old English and signed by the institute staff, were given to those who had taken the courses.

The knowledge and wisdom our Vietnamese teachers absorbed and retained is one thing that will be lasting, one thing no one can take away from them.

Social Services

The most diversified aspect of Salvation Army service in Vietnam was demonstrated by the social services unit. Those assigned to this team pursued their tasks with flair and professionalism. As supervisor, Captain Adele Meissner, with her knowledge and wide experience, contributed tremendously to the structuring and implementation of the program. Captain Jean Smith had both nursing and social services backgrounds, enabling her to be a liaison between our medical and social service programs. One of the duties of the social services staff was to work closely with the mobile medical clinics in the refugee camps. Referrals to social services were made by the doctors and nurses. For the majority of clinic patients, medical care was not all they were given. Through the social services unit they were also provided with home visitation and interview, transportation and accompaniment to hospital and/or treatment facilities, collection of reports from hospitals and laboratories, explanation of diagnosis, treatment, and medicines; distribution of food, medicine, and clothing; education in public health principles, and provision of progress reports to families of hospitalized patients.

Both private and clinical referrals were afforded the same services. Special attention and frequent follow-up were given to the families suffering from tuberculosis and other communicable diseases.

The medical/social phase played an extremely influential and often critical role in the total efficiency of Salvation Army services. One day while the 36th medical detachment of dentists was working in conjunction with our clinic, a mother brought a five-year-old girl for a tooth extraction. One look at the little girl's blue face and knotty fingers revealed clearly that she had a heart condition; hence, the dentist refused to extract the tooth. However, it was possible to refer the girl to the Salvation Army clinic, where the doctor contacted the social worker and referred her to a cardiologist, who accepted her case and performed the heart surgery shortly thereafter.

Even with a large qualified team, including Vietnamese counterparts who were being trained alongside of them, the social services staff had their hands full, often overextending themselves physically. In the morning you might see Captain Meissner in the office working diligently developing a program for day care centers; in the afternoon she could be out in the rural areas, teaching farmers how to grow vegetables. She also introduced many social service concepts that were new to the Vietnamese, such as more sophisticated types of recordkeeping and home visitation (the latter was not a cultural custom in Vietnam), and these were met with good acceptance.

The city of Saigon had a rehabilitation/detention center called Chanh Hung that housed an average of 200 inmates, aged 10-78--people who exhibited "anti-social" behavior patterns. Orphaned street boys, pickpockets, beggars, prostitutes, draft dodgers, curfew violators, and opium addicts were among the many types of "problems" dumped there. Others who probably shouldn't have been there at all were unclassified individuals, such as a confused school student or a bewildered war widow. The Chanh Hung population was often referred to by the Vietnamese as "the trash of Saigon." and when The Salvation Army began a work there, the Vietnamese were nicknaming the center *TeBan*, which means literally "no money, no parents."

Barbed wire and armed guards surrounded these outcasts, and their quarters had absolutely no furnishings beyond bare, concrete slabs on which they slept without any type of mat or covering. Bugs crawled the walls. From the repulsive smell, it was quite obvious where the inmates relieved themselves. No water was provided for them to wash their hands on hot days.

The only activities for the detainees were eating, sleeping, gambling, and smoking opium. Mealtime was their only opportunity to leave the four walls where they were confined. The entire male group occupied one room, the females another; this proved detrimental to rehabilitation since the older ones were a bad influence on the younger ones as they taught them "skills."

Rice was the main menu, but even that was of a low quality. (One teacher described it as the grade of rice fed to pigs.) Occasionally hot broth containing green vegetables was served, and--far too infrequently--fish. The food was prepared under less than desirable conditions, too.

The Vietnamese government gave the center 30 *piasters* (equivalent to about 10 cents in U.S. money) to take care of one inmate for one day.

No wonder many agencies had come--once--but never came back!

The mayor of Saigon, Colonel Mhieu, who was also in the Vietnamese military, expressed deep anxiety over the outrageous conditions. So much money had to be put toward the war, there just wasn't much left over for these unfortunates.

In desperation, the mayor requested to see Major Collins and personally took him on a tour through the center. Moved by the inmates and their needs, Major Collins authorized Salvation Army services to accept the challenge in April 1969. Our social services staff developed the program and began spending the bulk of their time and energy at Chanh Hung. Captain Erich Hamm set up organizational patterns and procured supplies. Eventually all three of our teams--medical, social services, and youth--became involved.

Paint and elbow grease quickly gave Chanh Hung a new face. Sanitation problems were attacked head on. Our staff grouped the inmates by ages and sex, and housed them accordingly. They purchased colorful mats so that each inmate could sleep more comfortably. They also supplied sufficient clothing for each person.

At the top of the priority list was giving each inmate a complete physical by a doctor. Varied indeed were the types of illnesses. Some inmates had the usual headache, belly cramps, etc.; others had more severe problems. One frail, rather lifeless young boy, age 16, had been picked up by a policeman because he failed to produce identification. Authorities considered him a draft dodger, not being certain of his age. He said he had no parents. Dr. Li Sin Wah gave him a complete physical, and with an extended examination, her suspicions were confirmed: he had tuberculosis. Mrs. Collins had him referred to one of the sanitariums, where we made daily visits to encourage him.

The medical team ran into some other problems, humorous in a way, but still cause for alarm. They had to be extremely careful with the distribution of oral medicines. One day Mrs. Captain Erich Hamm gave a patient enough medicine for the day, but when he left the clinic, he shared it with all his friends. Other patients found extreme delight in swapping theirs--a blue pill for a red one.

Many inmates could not read or write so the youth team instituted low-level classes. It wasn't easy for many of the students to concentrate on academic study: they had been used to a school-free lifestyle for too long. But they really gave our vocational instruction their full attention. The younger ones took great pride in the daily handicrafts they were permitted to make, and they would take their creations back to their rooms, adding to the decor.

An intensified recreational program proved to be of limitless value. It was a good outlet for displaced hostilities, and tired bodies were much easier to cope with at night.

On our premise that people who can follow the rules of games can also learn to live by the rules which govern society, we organized a Ping-Pong tournament. This gave the inmates another chance to take pride in their skills. Two teams, with six people on each, signed up to compete.

Hoang Thuat, our recreation director, organized the tournament with polished professionalism--not forgetting a thing. He had badges for the players, festive decorations, flags flying, an elaborate scoreboard, homemade grandstand seats, and even the final touch of background music.

From the very first blow of the ref's whistle, excitement reigned! The keenness and timing of the players gave evidence of the many hours they had practiced, and their eagerness to win showed true spirit. It was a fair game all the way, and the best man did win. Those who lost, did so like true sports. All the players tried so hard that we wanted to make every one a winner. Chanh Hung Vietnamese officials were present in full force and joined in the enthusiasm of the day. The chief of Chanh Hung, a policeman named Le Van Minh, presented the champion with his medal--a lovely Ping-Pong medallion strung on wide ribbon bearing the Vietnamese traditional colors of red and yellow. To both the winner and runner-up, Major Collins presented purse money. Soft drinks and bags of goodies were distributed to all participants.

The by-product of the tournament was most rewarding, going far beyond the walls of Chanh Hung. Six months after the contest, I was walking down the main street in Saigon when I heard someone behind me call out, "Madam! Hello, Madam!" Looking around, I discovered it was our Ping-Pong champion, clean and neat carrying a shoe-shine kit. He had been able to leave the center and start a booming business!

While coordinating all the activities at Chanh Hung, our social services team also made an in-depth study of each inmate, developing a full case history for the files by meeting each person on a one-to-one basis. This alone was a monumental task, considering the varied backgrounds.

Solutions to some to their cases involved locating family relatives. Often this meant countless hours of traveling throughout the country, and often trips were fruitless searches. One such incident involved Tran Tinh, a 13-year-old boy who by American standards looked about eight years old and was in "fair" physical condition. He had lived with his parents until he was seven. After his two older brothers died, he had been sent to live with his grandmother. Three months later he moved to his uncle's, and six weeks after that, his uncle had been killed on patrol. The lad was given 50 *piasters* and sent to Saigon alone. The police had picked him up, which is how he entered the center. His relatives insisted his parents were dead; they said there was just a grandmother left. Tran Tinh and a social worker flew up-country to find her, but to no avail. They left a message with a radio station in hopes that a reply might come through. The boy was brought back to Saigon and stayed with Major and Mrs. Collins until further arrangements could be made.

Through the medium of the social services team, additional vocational classes were given at Chanh Hung, including one on farming which really "took roots." This gave the inmates a foundation to build on when they would leave the center.

In efforts to cover all bases, Captain Meissner developed a job-placement bureau that afforded additional security for those being released. Many in the center were allowed early release, and she made every attempt to help them find a home on the outside with better living conditions. Some of the more enterprising inmates didn't need much help. Captain Meissner said she would never forget the six young women placed in Chanh Hung because they were suspected of selling and buying contraband. Before they entered the center, these young women had invested 50,000 *piasters* in contraband that was to come in on a Chinese ship. They were very concerned about losing their money, worth approximately 500 American dollars so the night before the ship was due, they took a concrete post and smashed a hole in the concrete wall of their room, escaping to meet the ship. They proved they could help themselves and arranged their own "early release"!

After the transformation of the center, when all programs had reached top momentum, The Salvation Army planned an open house at Chanh Hung, with much ceremonial regalia. The center looked sharp. All the inmates voluntarily spruced up. Fresh flowers and table covers accented the meeting area. The mayor of Saigon came with all the city officials and dignitaries, as well as prominent heads of the U.S. Agency for International Development. The mayor revealed his sympathy for his people in a surprise speech to inmates, challenging them to improve their lot even further. In an overabundance of gratitude for Salvation Army services, the mayor concluded by saying, "Many agencies came to Chanh Hung, but never returned. The Salvation Army came, but they returned-- again and again. Not only did they come back--they *did* something!"

When the war was winding down and The Salvation Army left Vietnam, the chief of Chanh Hung attempted to keep us there forever. In desperation he wrote to the mayor, listing all the names of the Salvation Army team, and he stated, "This agency cannot be replaced. They breathe the same air as the detainee, and because of the way they gave themselves, Chanh Hung has a new face, and for the first time, a successful program. They have given hope to the lives of these waifs and courage to make something of their lives. I hope this agency will be allowed to continue to work, planting the seeds of love in the hearts of the detainees. They need this agency."

By that time Salvation Army services weren't in Vietnam to receive this praise, or the publicity, but it was gratifying to learn the value placed on our ministry.

A few of our Vietnamese counterparts did continue at Chanh Hung, as I found out in a letter I received from Loan dated December 1974. She stressed that Xinh was still at Chanh Hung, still executing the teaching and training she had learned from us.

WORLD DISARMAMENT AND PEACE

Full Title: National Commander Addresses
United Nations General Assembly on Disarmament

By Andrew S. Miller

From "The War Cry"

Published by
The Salvation Army
National Headquarters
Verona, N.J., USA (July 30, 1988)

I come to you in the name and spirit of our Saviour and Lord Jesus Christ, the Prince of Peace, and on behalf of the international leader of The Salvation Army, General Eva Burrows.

In 1983, General Jarl Wahlström, then the International Leader of The Salvation Army, issued a Statement on World Disarmament and Peace, which was sent to the United Nations and was graciously acknowledged and welcomed by the secretary-general. The position of The Salvation Army under General Burrows remains constant and is committed to the basic concepts of that historic document. While men and women of goodwill everywhere are grateful for the current signs of hope as the super-powers continue fruitful negotiations, we feel it remains important to reiterate what The Salvation Army said five years ago. The Salvation Army therefore:

1. *Renews* our plea to the United Nations Organization to strenuously maintain its efforts for world peace, and Member States to fulfill their obligation to abide by the provisions of the United Nations Charter, to seek the resolution of disputes by peaceful means, and to refrain from the threat or use of force in any manner inconsistent with the purposes of the United Nations;

2. *Calls on* all governments to reduce their total weapon capability to the minimum level necessary for present security;

3. *Continues to urge* world leaders to take positive action to remove causes of mistrust, fear, tension and hostility, to strengthen institutions for maintaining peace, and to show a determination to move toward elimination of the specter of nuclear conflict which still imperils civilization;

4. *Recommends* again that in a world of finite resources, benefits to be derived from reallocation of excessive military expenditure be identified, and the sharing of these resources for development programs at home and abroad be planned in good faith, with

special regard to alleviating world hunger, poverty, and removing the deep scars of human suffering.

The Salvation Army reaffirms its beliefs in the love of God for all peoples, and in the standards of righteousness and justice set forth in the Bible and revealed to mankind in Jesus Christ as the basis for harmonious interpersonal and international relationships.

Salvationists everywhere pledge themselves to continue to pray for peace, and gladly join all Christians in seeking to revitalize the Church's unique witness to the source of true peace, God Himself. They will strive to exemplify convincingly the

Christ-like spirit of brotherly love, mutual concern, and honesty in all their relationships. This, we feel, is a positive and distinctive contribution to the peace of the world.

Today, General Burrows pledges the moral resources of more than two and one-half million Salvationists throughout the world to world disarmament, peace on earth, goodwill to men.

VI. Despair

William Booth points out that victims of "the hopeless river of despair" are not limited to the poor.

"No matter whether their lot be one of wealth or poverty, prosperity or adversity, success or failure," he wrote, "they find difficulties connected with it, which bring a weight upon their spirits and a sadness to their hearts, clouding them with gloom, and making them, ever and anon, long to die."

Declaring that they often try to keep up appearances, he describes them as "smirking and smiling with their countenance, and uttering hypocrisies about happiness with their lips, while they are inwardly wishing that they had never been born, or even striving to summon courage to put an end to their lives."

For such people, Booth declares, "Salvation will immediately lift the load from his heart; and though, for a season, his trials may be as heavy as ever, it will bear him up amidst them all."

Despair (from *Darkest England*)

When we are snugly tucked into our own beds, we are apt to forget the multitudes outside in the rain and the storm who are shivering the long hours through on the hard stone seats in the open or under the arches of the railway. These homeless, hungry people are, however, there, but being broken-spirited folk for the most part they seldom make their voices audible in the ears of their neighbors. Now and again, however, a harsh cry from the depths is heard for a moment, jarring rudely upon the ear, and then all is still. (page 38)

Lazarus showed his rags and his sores too conspicuously for the convenience of Dives, and was summarily dealt with in the name of law and order. But as we have Lord Mayor's Days, when all the well-fed fur-clad City Fathers in State Coaches go through town, why should we not have a Lazarus Day, in which the starving Out-of-Works, and the sweated half-starved "In-Works" of London should crawl in their tattered raggedness, with their gaunt, hungry faces, and emaciated wives and children, a Procession of Despair through the main thoroughfares, past the massive houses and princely palaces of luxurious London?

For these men are gradually, but surely, being sucked down into the quicksand of modern life. They stretch out their grimy hands to us in vain appeal, not for charity, but for work.

(page 39)

THE ABANDONED CHILD

By S. Carvosso Gauntlett

From "Social Evils the Army Has Challenged"

Published by
Salvationist Publishing and Supplies
London (1946)

General Bramwell Booth, in the last chapter but one of his book, *Echoes and Memories,* tells of one problem in the presence of which he always felt dumb.

> *"It is the problem of suffering children. I cannot grasp anything tangible in the Divine purpose which permits little children to suffer. I cannot doubt His love. I know that wisdom belongeth to Him. All the same, I feel, not merely pain, but a sense of profound mystery when I approach the suffering of children. I hear above the voice of the crippled and starved another voice which stirs me. I am in the presence of the insoluble. I realize this in connection with those states of misery of the innocent and helpless, as I do not realize it even in experiences which might be thought more solemn, such as the presence of death or of widespread calamity."*

That passage explains the passion with which the Army's second General, when still a young man, threw himself into the fight against the abuse of small girls and the poignancy of some of his letters of those days. No doubt it also explains his earnest efforts on behalf of "the Abandoned Child."

In 1908 a Bill was brought before the House of Commons which was to amend the Industrial Schools Act of 1866 and 1880, by making the provisions of those Acts, regarding "the setting up and maintenance of Industrial Schools, and the committal to them of children found in certain circumstances, compulsory instead of permissive."

Drafted by Bramwell Booth, the Bill was backed by a number of influential Members of Parliament. These included T. P. O'Connor, Atherly Jones, K. C., F. E. Smith, K. C. (later Lord Chancellor and first Earl of Birkenhead), and Ramsay MacDonald (years later to become Prime Minister).

A notable and in parts terrible book--*The Abandoned Child*--was issued by the Army's International Headquarters for private circulation among Members of Parliament and other influential personages. It contained a statesmanlike plea by Bramwell Booth, at that time Chief of the Staff of The Salvation Army; The Print of the Bill; and "An Appeal to All Lovers of Children" based on thorough investigations made by the Army into conditions in many parts of Britain. The language of this latter document at times departs from the sober tone one would expect in a book of this kind; obviously the horrors disclosed, and the helplessness or indifferences of the authorities, had made a deep impression on the writer's mind and heart.

In 1908, 5,000 children of tramps were estimated to be continually "on the road," with consequences to their health, education and morals which can be only partly imagined. Among cases cited by Bramwell Booth in his introduction to the book are those of a tramp, all of whose seven children had been born "upon the road;" and of two little girls living with their mother in a house of ill fame: the mother had been repeatedly imprisoned for neglect or cruelty, but each time, on her release, *the children had been handed back to her!*

The book quotes a speech by Sir William Treloar, at one time Lord Mayor of the City of London:

> *"One of the most terrible sights I ever see as a magistrate* (said Sir William) *is the sight of a big policeman bringing before me little boys of eight and ten years, charged with the crime of wandering. That means the policeman found them, perhaps at three or four o'clock on a winter's morning, walking about wet through, shoeless, ragged, hungry, trying probably to eat a cabbage-stalk to keep their little bodies and souls together. It is from such as these we get our cripples."*

To this latter statement, the Army's investigator added:

> *"Ay, and far worse even than cripples, too; far worse! For he might have spoken of little girls-- little girls who share equally in all the misery that befalls their brothers; and, in addition to that, are the victims of horrors unspeakable, of outrage, such as one cannot think without shuddering, such as Sir William could not mention at a public gathering."*

171

The 5,000 "children of the road" were but a small part of the host of endangered childhood whom Bramwell Booth and his helpers had in mind. It was estimated that 30,000 children ought at once to be sent to Industrial Schools. The book suggested that it would be better to relieve the parents of their responsibility for these children than to allow the boys and girls to become an army of criminals, loafers and outcasts.

The Salvationists agreed with the chief constable of a large seaside town who had declared that it was a very good thing to lift up men and women as the Army was doing, but far better still to take a child by the hand and prevent it from falling.

The published report of the Army's investigator--a "toned-down" summary of the original, which contained stories almost incredible, and not fit to be read by the general public--is crowded with sickening examples of "children of all ages not merely living in the same house with the most degraded of fallen creatures, but occupying the same rooms--the same bed."

In the presence of such a problem, Bramwell Booth must indeed have felt "a sense of profound mystery." But, as many times before, perplexity led him and the Army to take action.

Back in 1866--forty years before the Salvationist agitation began--Parliament had recognized the need for protecting endangered children and had passed the Industrial Schools Bill. Industrial Schools were to rescue such children. They could also be used as a means of punishing youthful offenders--this being regarded as a necessary part of the rescue work; though a clear distinction was made between that and their primary object.

The Elementary Education Act of 1870 empowered education authorities to send truants to Industrial Schools. Alas! the new use soon overwhelmed the earlier purpose. By the beginning of the twentieth century, the redemptive function of the Schools, as The Salvation Army's inquiries disclosed, had ceased almost everywhere. In large towns and cities, as well as in small places, the Army's investigator had found the same conditions: practically nothing was being done under the Industrial Schools Act; all was done under the Education Act. In the densely populated as in the sparsely peopled counties, no children were being considered, except school truants.

Moreover, even in the few places where something was being done for boys, the authorities had "nothing for girls"!

Many parts of the country had not adopted the Act at all. Elsewhere it had been put into operation only because officers of the National Society for the Prevention of Cruelty to Children had managed to make their influences irresistible.

The main defect--which the Bill sponsored by The Salvation Army set out to remedy--was that the Industrial Schools Act was only *permissive.*

Bramwell Booth pointed out that under the Act of 1866, "any person" *might* bring a child of under fourteen years--"found begging, wandering without home or proper guardianship, destitute, having parents in prison, who frequents the company of thieves, or who lives with or frequents the company of prostitutes"--before a Justice of the Peace, and the latter *might* commit the child to an Industrial School.

The Army proposed to impose on education authorities as well as on the police the obligation to bring such a child before the court. And the court, in turn, if its inquiry showed that the child should be dealt with under the proposed Act, *should*--not *might*, as previously--order him to be sent to an Industrial School.

Magistrates were to be empowered to issue search warrants, so that houses of ill-fame might be entered and children searched for and removed, as magistrates were already empowered to act under the Prevention of Cruelty to Children Act.... This provision would mainly affect brothels.

It was further proposed to make it *compulsory* on the education authorities to provide any needed Industrial School accommodation, as it was to provide elementary schools.

Under the old system, as the Army's investigator stated, whenever a child was brought before them, many local authorities adopted a very simple means of procedure. The clerk was asked two short questions and gave two even shorter answers.

"Will it cost us anything?"

"Yes."

"Are we obliged to do it?"

"No."

And here it often ended. Whatever happened, the rates must not go up!

The result was a gross inequality as between different towns. London, though far from perfect, ever since the passing of the 1886 Act had supported a staff of Industrial School officers, and according to the latest reports had sent 752 children to Industrial Schools. Liverpool, with about one-seventh of London's population, sent 616. On the other hand, Manchester and Salford, whose combined population was nearly 80,000 greater than Liverpool's, sent only about 100 children--one sixth the number of Liverpool. Birmingham sent 120, Glasgow, 165, and Edinburgh only 21. In many districts absolutely nothing was done.

If all the country were worked as well as Birmingham, it was pointed out, the total of 4,061 would have been 10,000; if as well as London and Liverpool together, 14,000. If the country had received the same care as was given to Liverpool, the total of 4,061 would have mounted to 30,000!

Against the criminal reluctance of many authorities to spend money on the rescue of endangered children, General Bramwell Booth used this notable argument:

"If, as has been recently stated on high authority, a child at birth is worth £5 to the State, and a skilled mechanic at twenty-five is worth £200 to the State, then it is obviously to the interest of the country that a child who is in danger of

becoming a pauper, thief, hooligan, or unemployable, should be rescued so as to make it an asset instead of a burden. In this connection it may be mentioned that 90 percent of the girls who have left Industrial Schools during the last three years, and 86 per cent of the boys, are now in permanent employment. It is submitted that the money spent on these children has been a good investment, for if it had not been spent, the majority of them would probably have cost infinitely more to keep in workhouses and prisons."

What of the *results* of the Army's plea and its effort in Parliament?

The Bill drafted by Bramwell Booth passed the first reading and, while it encountered some criticism, its main clauses were accepted by the Under Secretary for Home Affairs--Mr. Herbert (now Viscount) Samuel. These clauses were included in the Government's own Bill, which--known as "The Children's Charter"--became law in the same year, 1908.

At this distance, it is of some interest to recall a few of the effects of the legislation resulting from the Army's agitation:

A parent, or any other person who has charge of a child under five years of age, may be fined a sum not exceeding £3 if he gives the child intoxicating liquor, except upon the orders of a doctor or in case of sickness or other urgent cause. A mother, even if she be a temperate women, who allows her child to sip from the glass of beer she is taking is liable to punishment. In the interests of children every citizen should see that this law is carried out.

Parents ill-treating or neglecting their children can be punished, if the ill-treatment or neglect causes or is likely to cause actual suffering or injury to health.

Children of drunken and criminal parents--and they must number many thousands--can also be sent to an Industrial School. If this clause of the Act is vigorously carried out, large numbers of such children may be saved from becoming drunkards or criminals.

Children living in houses of ill-fame, and associating with immoral women, can also be rescued.

A pamphlet published by The Salvation Army after the passing of the Act--more especially for the guidance of its Officers--concluded with this passage:

> *"Many of the offenses for which children can be rescued are in no sense crimes. It is not a crime, for instance, to be the child of a drunken, criminal, or immoral parent; or to associate with thieves.*
>
> *"It will, therefore, be necessary to strengthen the hands of the police, by bringing cases to their notice and assisting them in every possible way. If any citizen sees a crime being committed, his first impulse is to run for the police, so that the criminal may be arrested. He is bound to do this, or come under the penalty of the law; he is also bound, if called upon in the King's name, to assist the police in the apprehension of the criminal. Is it not as important to save a child as to punish crime?"*

Every officer was called upon in the name of Christ to save His little ones from the road that would ultimately lead them to the abyss of vice, misery and crime. Just as no officer would see a little child drown without attempting to rescue it, or see a baby starve for want of a little bread and milk, so no officer would allow a child to be ruined in body and soul without doing his utmost to save it from perdition.

In the thirty-odd years since then [1946], Salvationists throughout the land have done much to abolish the social evil against which this particular challenge was directed.

A THIRD OPINION

By Bob Scott

From "The War Cry"

Published by
The Salvation Army
National Headquarters
Verona, N.J., USA (June 24, 1989)

There's a woman in a window
Sitting all alone.
She does not see her neighbors
Or hear her telephone.

She is thinking of a nurse
At a clinic in the town,
Listening to a girl
Whose head is hanging down.

The girl says, "I'm ashamed."
She says, "And I'm afraid
My parents will not understand
The mistake that I have made.

"They think that I'm a good girl.
They even think I'm smart.
But if I have this baby,
It will break my mother's heart."

The nurse writes down her name
And nods a time or two.
Then calmly she explains
What the girl should do.

"You are really very young.
You will have other babies, dear.
It's just a routine procedure
And nothing you should fear."

The woman in the window
Looks back twenty years ago,
Across the miles and memories,
At all the things she did not know.

That her parents really loved her,
And how fast the years go by,
And how "routine procedures"
Sometimes go awry.

Tears well up in the woman's eyes
For a life she never knew,
For children she could never have
And things she would never do.

She'd never buy a teddy bear
For a daughter or a son,
Or kiss a hurt to make it well
Or watch her children run.

She'd never make a birthday cake
Where a single candle shone,
Or draw a mark on her kitchen door
To show how a child had grown.

She'd never join a PTA,
Or help at a school bazaar
Or chauffeur kids to Little League
In an overcrowded car.

She'd never hear her children pray,
Or say their "ABCs",
Or stuff their Christmas stockings
Or trim their Christmas trees.

She'd never sign a report card,
Or give her kids a bath,
Or watch them build a treehouse
Or smile when she heard them laugh.

There's a woman in a window
Sitting all alone.
She does not see her neighbors
Or hear her telephone.

SHE LIGHTS CANDLES

By Dorothy Hughes Post

From "The War Cry"

Published by
The Salvation Army
National Headquarters
Verona, N.J., USA (February 4, 1989)

There is the New York City tourists see and enjoy--
the World Trade Towers, the Statue of Liberty and
Rockefeller Center. There is also the elegant New York
City where fashionable people enjoy a Broadway musical
or dine at the Four Seasons.

There is another New York, visible mainly at night.
It is peopled by prostitutes, transvestites, welfare hotel
residents, the homeless, pimps and drug dealers. Danger
surrounds these New Yorkers like a mine field ready to
explode.

People on the streets are victims in one way or
another. Most endured an unhappy childhood, the targets
of child abuse. Deprived of any self-esteem, they believe
there are no other choices for them.

For the past four years, another face has become
familiar to the dwellers of darkness. It is the face of
Major Betty Baker at the window of a Salvation Army
canteen. She criss-crosses New York's West Side nightly,
with her driver and dog, between 10 p.m. and 4 a.m. She
dispenses hot or cold drinks and cookies to street people,
along with lively conversation in a Scottish brogue. When
she can, she provides hats, gloves, blankets, food packages
and toilet articles.

This ministry began as a dream of Lt. Colonel Clarence
Kinnett, then Greater New York divisional commander.
His successor, Colonel Wallace Conrath, told Major Baker
that they had looked over the records of every officer in
the New York area, and she was best suited for this
demanding work. She accepted the assignment as an
appointment from God.

Her own experiences have prepared her for this work.
When she was just 21, her husband deserted her while she
was in the hospital. A personal encounter with God's love
healed the pain and compelled her to share that love with
others--especially the forgotten and hopeless.

Major Baker is a unique blend of assertiveness and
tenderness. She is street-wise and sometimes talks tough,
but her people know that she would move heaven and
earth to help them. The question is, does her presence in
the darkness make a difference?

She serves hot chocolate and cookies. What possible difference can that make to people who dwell in darkness, surrounded by evil and danger?

But Major Betty Baker's presence on the streets of New York City each night *does* make a difference in the lives of the prostitutes, transvestites and street people who make up her flock. Her ministry is a candle that pierces the night with a ray of hope.

In the four and-a-half years she has devoted to this work, she has been honored by a variety of organizations. In 1987, *Woman's Day* magazine recognized her as an Outstanding Woman "for responding selflessly to the needs of the street people of New York with caring and dedication and in the process, helping to make our world more decent and humane."

Such honors are rewarding. But it is the tributes of street people themselves that please her most. They are proof that her work is not in vain.

"You know, I really believe in God," one such man said to her one night. "That's nice," she commented. "It really helps and strengthens you when you believe in Him."

His reply left her speechless. "You don't understand. I believe in God because I see Him in you!"

A 34 year-old drug runner calls her "a breath of fresh air." And Twinkles, a 40 year-old transvestite, says that talking to Major Baker is like coming into "air conditioned comfort in an overheated situation."

He recalls the first time he met Major Baker, he was suspicious. Who was she and what was she doing on the streets? He thought she was an evangelist who would preach at him. But, as he discovered, "She's a *friend*. I look forward to seeing her every night."

Her nights are not always so rewarding. Often evil seems overwhelming. Her *girls* live in constant danger. The longer they are on the streets, the greater is the chance they will die at the hands of a customer, their pimps, or as a result of a sexually transmitted disease.

In the past four years, at least 23 prostitutes have been murdered in the section of New York she serves. Most of them had stopped at Major Baker's canteen for coffee and conversation.

Major Baker grieves over each of those girls as if they were her own. One girl's death nearly caused her to give up. Eve spoke to her the night she was stabbed to death. She seemed ready to leave the streets. Unfortunately, Major Baker did not learn of Eve's death until after her funeral, so she was unable to assist with the arrangements.

Major Baker was so angry that she felt she could no longer continue in a ministry that seemed so futile. To ease her frustration, she picked up her accordion and began to play. She found herself singing a Salvation Army song by Will Brand:

> By the love that never ceased to hold me,
> By the blood which thou didst shed for me,
> While thy presence and thy power enfold me,
> I renew my covenant with thee.

She was reminded of the moment she became aware of God's great love for her. His presence washed away her anger and pain. She experienced His love and healing again that night as she renewed her covenant to serve Him on the streets of New York.

That moment deepened her commitment, but has not ended her feelings of concern and frustration. Occasionally, she learns that a girl has returned home to the *straight life* because of something she did or said. And last spring a transvestite invited her to attend his college graduation. He left that lifestyle largely because of her influence.

More typically, however, street people remain on the streets, even with the dangers involved. It is frustrating for Major Baker to watch people remain in situations that are self-destructive. In addition to the threat of physical violence, AIDS is a special danger to prostitutes, transvestites and drug users. In spite of these risks, the excitement of life on the streets becomes so addictive that many are unable to leave.

A policeman once spoke with Major Baker about the men and women she serves. "These people won't change," he said. "You got that right," she replied, "but I know Someone who *can* change them!"

Her faith in God's ability to work miracles in people's lives is undaunted. She speaks of the need for a safe house for prostitutes and another for transvestites. She realizes that in most cases transvestites cannot be treated in 90 days, since their lifestyles have evolved over a long period of time. "But," she says, "we can never discount the grace of God."

Her faith in God enables her to see beyond the exterior of the people who live on the streets of New York. "I've never seen such pitiful people," she says, "but even if they are difficult, they are made in the image of God."

Because she recognizes the image of God in each of her people, she treats them with respect. She does not preach at them, though she longs to get them off the street to safety. Most of the time, she simply listens. "Sometimes I think I'm a mother these kids never had, someone they can talk to."

When the opportunity arises, however, she is quick to point out that there is a better way and to encourage them to choose that way.

With all the frustration and disappointment of her work, Major Baker still feels strongly that her appointment is from God. "I think that for some of them I am the only part of God that can really touch them. To know that I am part of God's plan for their lives is great."

VII. Atheism

General Booth sees Atheism, with its denial of the very existence of God, as the epitome of evil, and the source of many of the dark rivers of human misery.

He writes, "The last river, the blackest, and the most productive of misery, both here and hereafter, is Atheism, with its senseless unbelief, and daring blasphemies."

But there is hope for the unbeliever. "If he has experienced the influence of the atheistic system," says the General, "Salvation will bring to his soul the realization that God lives; and the assurance that God lives in him will disperse every figment of his former unbelief."

In the intervening years, multitudes have found new life through faith in a Living Christ, as Salvationists have proclaimed the Gospel, and witnessed to their faith.

Atheism (from *Darkest England*)

To get a man soundly saved, it is not enough to put on him a pair of new breeches, or give him regular work, or even to give him a University education. These things are all outside a man, and if the inside remains unchanged you have wasted your labor. You must in some way or other graft upon the man's nature a new nature, which has in it the element of the Divine. All that I propose in this book is governed by that principle.   (page 53)

"God is Love." Was it not, then, the accents of God's voice that sounded there above the din of the street and the swearing of the slums? Yea, verily, and that voice ceased not and will not cease, so long as the Slum Sisters fight under the banner of The Salvation Army.

To form an idea of the immense amount of good, temporal and spiritual, which the Slum Sister is doing, you need to follow them into the kennels where they live, preaching the Gospel with the mop and the scrubbing brush, and driving out the devil with soap and water.
(page 173)

While using all material means, our reliance is on the co-working of God. We keep our powder dry, but we trust in Jehovah. We go not forth in our own strength to this battle; our dependence is upon Him who can influence the heart of man. There is no doubt that the most satisfactory method of raising a man must be to effect such a change in his views and feelings that he shall voluntarily abandon his evil ways, give himself to industry and goodness in the midst of the very temptations and companionship that before led him astray, and live a Christian life, an example in himself of what can be done by the power of God in the very face of the most impossible circumstances.   (page 249)

A RISING TIDE OF ATHEISM, AND OUR DEFENSE AGAINST IT

By Samuel Logan Brengle

From "The Staff Review"

Published by
The Salvation Army
International Headquarters
London (January 1928)

A wide knowledge of history tends to sanity, to sobriety, and correctness of judgment of men and events, if only we have seen God in history. We need such knowledge to give us perspective, to steady us, to save us from snap judgments, to insure us against cocksureness on one hand and despair on the other. Without this wide, long view we are not unlike a tiny boat on a tempestuous sea, tossed like a ship on the waves, but with it we are more like a great ship that rides serenely over the billows.

To the casual observer, the experience of the race seems tidal, always flowing and ebbing like the tides of the sea; or forever moving in a circle, getting nowhere, evermore coming back from whence it started, like rivers rising out of and returning to the oceans. The

> "One far-off divine event,
> To which the whole creation moves,"

and the slow, but sure workings of Providence and the unfailing purpose and process of the Divine government are hidden from him.

When I was a child on the wide, bare, unprotected prairies of the Middle West, black clouds and fierce thunderstorms filled me with anxious fears and vague terror, but as I grew to manhood I saw them as a part of a vast and ordered whole, and they lost their power to create panic in me.

Once when sick and prostrated in health I was thrown into a state of mental and spiritual anxiety, amounting almost to torture, by the nation-wide excitement over a great prize-fight. I felt our American civilization was only veneered barbarism, and for a time it seemed to me that we were reverting to, and were to be swallowed up by, brutal, sensuous paganism; then, on my knees, praying, I remembered the days when *not one but a thousand gladiators* fought each other to the death in the Coliseum, or battled and struggled with, and were devoured by, wild beasts to make a Roman holiday, while the mobs of the city by the hundred thousand, headed by the Emperor, senators, philosophers, noble ladies, and all the *élite* gloated over the cruel, bloody scene. Then in deep reverence and gratitude and glad trust I gave God thanks, as I saw how far He had led us on, and was still leading, from those ghastly pleasures, those merciless days.

When I was a child, the Civil War was raging; soldiers marched and counter-marched through our peaceful little valley and village; armies stormed and thundered across the land; proud cities were besieged and starved, and fell before conquering hosts; fathers, brothers, sons were perishing in bloody combat, in fetid swamps and prison camps; homes were vanishing; funeral bells were ever tolling; mothers, sisters, wives, and orphans were ever weeping, weeping; the foundations of the social order seemed to be crumbling, and men turned their thoughts to the apocalyptic portions of Scripture and tried to interpret the times by their symbolisms and turned their eyes to the clouds in expectation of the Saviour's bodily appearing, longing for Him to come and work out the Salvation which man himself--abasing his pride and yielding to the lordship of Jesus, under the leadership of the sanctifying Spirit--must work out for himself, or perish.

It was years before the light of history enabled me to escape this bald interpretation of apocalyptic symbols and walk in quietness and peace and close attention to daily duty, while a world quaked and trembled in unparalleled hurricanes of war, assured that "the heavens do rule," and "a Watcher and an Holy One" in the heavens was interested in our perplexity and sore travail and would guide us through the storm and tempest, purified and chastened, to a haven of peace.

History is repeating itself in spirit among us, and a very militant Society for the Propagation of Atheism has recently received letters of incorporation from the legislators of New York, and an Anti-Bible Society also has been incorporated. For its first year's budget this Anti-Bible Society is asking for $88,000, and offering life membership for $1,000. Its avowed object "is to discredit the Bible," to "make known its human origin, evolutionary formation, and its discreditable history; expose its immoral and barbaric contents; and lay bare its anti-scientific, anti-liberal, and irrational teachings." Such is the program it offers. It proposes to show that "the Bible is the work of man." "The falsification by deliberate mistranslation is the sole basis of orthodoxy." "The inhuman character of the Bible-God shall be offered in evidence against the Book." "The Bible patriarchs shall be shown to be a set of unmatched moral monsters." "The spirit of injustice and intolerance dominate the Bible." "The Sermon on the Mount consists mainly of romantic sentimentalism unrelated to reality." "The Bible is inimical to civilization. It must and shall be discredited." "The American Anti-Bible Society has no religious tests for membership, except disbelief in the Bible as divinely inspired." "Help us free America from Bible-bondage."

These are some tidbits from its bulletin or manifesto. The Society for the Propagation of Atheism has already enlisted many young people and students, and societies of "damned souls," as they dub themselves, are flourishing in many of our American schools and colleges. It is all a part of a nationwide, worldwide movement; the wash of wide, sweeping waves of Atheism gushing forth from the heart of the Russian Revolution; something that the Army and all lovers of our Lord and of the Bible will have to face and possibly come into close and desperate grips with in the near future.

If these gentlemen were better acquainted with history they might not be so cocksure of discrediting the Bible and banishing God from His throne. If we are acquainted with history and the Bible we shall not be uncertain as to the final issue, but neither will we sit down in a fool's paradise and think we can drive back the waves of mocking, irresponsible, desperate unbelief and save the rising generation from its desolating menace by witty retort, by smart rejoinder, or by learned and masterly debate.

*　*　*

How shall we reply to this denial of the Divine elements of the Bible? How shall we prove it to be God-inspired? Is it a subject of *proof* or of *faith*? How can I be sure of it for myself? and how can I prove it to others? Paul says, "All Scripture is given by inspiration of God," but that is an assertion, not a proof. It still has to be proved, if it can be.

I had studied the various arguments for the inspiration of the Bible by theologians, and since I had from my infancy up accepted the Bible as God's book, they confirmed my unquestioning faith. But there came a time when I needed more than learned arguments to prove it to me. And not until God Himself came to my help was I wholly, invincibly convinced.

That which finally established my faith in the divinity of the Bible was opened eyes, an inner illumination of my own soul, which enables me to behold wondrous things all through its sacred pages. "Open Thou mine eyes that I may behold wondrous things out of Thy law," prayed the Psalmist. The book is largely sealed to men of unanointed eyes and self-satisfied, or world-satisfied, hearts, and from men who turn from the paths of rectitude and "stumble at the Word, being disobedient."

The final blessing that Jesus gave His disciples just before He ascended from them was the blessing of this inner illumination of opened eyes. "Then opened He their understanding, that they might understand the Scriptures" (Luke 24:45).

The sun does not need learned astronomical treatises to prove its existence, nor a candle of man's making to enable it to be seen. All it needs is that men should have eyes to see. It is its own evidence. So the Bible carries in itself evidences of inspiration. "I know the Bible is inspired," said a great soul-winner, "because it inspires me." What the sun is in the world of material things, that the Bible is in the world of spiritual things. It is a lamp to the feet, a light unto the path, of men whose spiritual eyes are open, and who will resolutely follow where it leads. Let us notice some of the assertations of the Book and find if they can be proved, not by argument, but by life, by experience, for the Bible is but a venerable and curious bit of ancient literature to be read for pleasure or to gratify curiosity, if it does not answer to the deep needs of life, the hunger of the soul, the fears, the hopes, the aspirations, the questionings of the spirit in man.

"Man shall not live by bread alone," said Jesus, "but by every word that proceedeth out of the mouth of God." Does the Bible feed the soul of man? All the saints and soldiers of Jesus of all the ages have been nourished and have lived on the Word of God.

"I have esteemed the words of His mouth more than my necessary food," said Job. "How sweet are Thy words unto my taste! Yea, sweeter than honey to my mouth,"

191

wrote the Psalmist. "More to be desired are they than gold, yea, than
much fine gold: sweeter also than honey and the honeycomb." "Thy words were found, and I did eat them," said Jeremiah. "And Thy Word was unto me the joy and rejoicing of my heart."

* * *

Does the Bible help men to live finer, cleaner, saintly lives? It certainly does. The man who receives the Word of God into his heart will stop sinning. "Thy Word have I hid in my heart that I might not sin against Thee," wrote the Psalmist. "Wherewithal shall a young man cleanse his way? by taking heed thereto according to Thy Word." "Sin shall not have dominion over you; for ye are not under the law, but under grace."

Does the Bible offer hope to the sinner? to the man who has wasted his life? or scorned the voice of conscience? or turned his back on light and goodness and God? It is the only Book in the world that does. It, and it alone, tells of a redeeming God, a Saviour from sin, a loving Heavenly Father who waits to welcome sinners.

"God commendeth His love toward us in that while we were yet sinners Christ died for us." "This is a faithful saying, and worthy of all acceptation, that Christ Jesus came into the world to save sinners." "If we confess our sins He is faithful and just to forgive us our sins and to cleanse us from all unrighteousness." Ten thousand times ten thousand sinners saved by faith in the Saviour revealed in the Bible will testify to the truth of those words.

Does the Bible offer succor to tempted men and women? Does it comprehend our need? It *does* as no other book in the world does. It reveals an elder Brother who enters into the fellowship of our temptations. "For in that He Himself hath suffered being tempted, He is able to succor them that are tempted" (Heb. 2:18); "For we have not an High Priest which cannot be touched with the feelings of our infirmities; but was in all points tempted like as we are, yet without sin" (Heb. 4:15); "God is faithful, who will not suffer you to be tempted above that ye are able; but will with the temptation also make a way to escape, that ye may be able to bear it" (1 Cor. 10:18).

Does the Bible tell men how to know the full sufficiency of this elder Brother? Here are His own words in answer: "If ye love Me, keep My commandments, and I will pray the Father, and He shall give you another Comforter that He may abide with you forever.... At that day ye shall know that I am in My Father, and ye in Me, and I in you.... All power is given unto Me in heaven and in earth.... Lo! I am with you alway even unto the end of the world."

Has the Bible any word for the toilers and burdened people of earth, the perplexed, the careworn? It has--sweet words of comprehension and assurance such as can nowhere else be found: "Come unto me, all ye that labor and are heavy laden, and I will give you rest. Take my yoke upon you, and learn of me; for I am meek and lowly in heart: and ye shall find rest unto your souls. For my yoke is easy and my burden is light."

Has the Bible any word for the persecuted, the maligned, the oppressed? Listen: "Blessed are they which are persecuted for righteousness' sake: for theirs is the kingdom of Heaven. Blessed are ye, when men shall revile you, and persecute you, and shall say all manner of evil against you falsely for My sake; Rejoice and be exceeding glad: for great is your reward in Heaven." "From Heaven did the Lord behold the earth; to hear the groaning of the prisoner; to loose those appointed to death."

Has the Bible any word for those who are sore afflicted? "He hath not despised nor abhorred the affliction of the afflicted; neither hath He turned away His face from him; but when he cried unto Him, He heard." "In all their affliction He was afflicted." "If we suffer we shall also reign with Him; for our light affliction worketh for us." Worketh what? "Worketh for us a far more exceeding and eternal weight of glory: while we look not at the things which are seen but at the things which are not seen." Hallelujah!

"For I reckon that the sufferings of this present time are not worthy to be compared with the glory which shall be revealed in us."

Has the Bible a word for those whose eyes are dim with tears? "God shall wipe away all tears from their eyes." For those who are in pain? "Neither shall there be any more pain."

Has it any word about the far future? "Blessed are the dead that die in the Lord: it doth not yet appear what we shall be: but we know that when He shall appear, we shall be like Him; for we shall see Him as He is; and God shall wipe away all tears; and there shall be no more death, neither sorrow nor crying."

* * *

HOW CAN I PROVE THE INSPIRATION OF THE BIBLE? *By the way it answers to the heart of man.* The key that fits an intricate lock was evidently made for that lock. The Bible meets me at every point of my moral and spiritual need; it fits my heart's intricate needs as the key fits the lock, and I doubt not, I exult to know that the Divine Hand that fashioned me gives me the Book, and His heart that loves me pours itself with fathomless comforts into my heart through the Book. But I can prove to others the divinity of the Book only in the same way that I can prove to them that the sun is shining, the honey is sweet, that the song of the bird is melodious--by inducing them to put my assertations to the test of experience.

The inspiration of the Bible is proved by experience, not by logic. "Meditate therein day and night" to obey, "to do according to all that is written therein," and you shall know, you shall taste its sweetness, behold its wonders, and hear in its words the whisperings of the everlasting Father to the heart of His child.

HOW SHALL I PROVE TO OTHERS, TO THOSE WHO QUESTION, WHO DOUBT, WHO DENY, THAT THE BIBLE IS A GOD-GIVEN, GOD-INSPIRED BOOK? Shall I go to history, science, archeology, for proof? Yes, at the proper time and to the right people. But the most convincing proof of inspiration of the Bible that I can offer to an unbeliever is a redeemed life, lived in the power and sweetness of the

Spirit; *a life that matches the Bible*; a life of love, of prayer and faith and devotion; a life of joy and peace and patience and sweet goodwill to all men; a life full of good works, matching a glad testimony to the saving, sanctifying, keeping power and ever living presence of the Lord Jesus; a life like that of a convert from heathenism, whose heathen neighbors said of him: *"There is no difference between you and the Book!"* He was a living Bible known and read of them all, and they saw and felt in him inspiration. He was inbreathed, indwelt of God, and through him they recognized inspiration in the Book.

Redeemed lives, drawing light and strength and inspiration from and matching the inspired Book, are the unanswerable proofs of its inspiration.

Dr. Grenfell, of Labrador, tells us that when a student in a University in England, he lived with a professor who was a lecturer on the evidences of Christianity. This lecturer was in frequent controversy with infidels, but never converted one of them. They would meet in public debate, each supported by his friends and followers, who were confirmed in their opinions, but there was no changing of sides, no converts were made. It was heady, a rivalry of wits, a struggle for mastery, an intellectual fisticuffs to no profit. But one day one of the most doughty of these infidel debaters was stricken with fatal illness. His friends had no words of comfort and left him to himself. Then a sweet, humble sister Salvationist stepped in and nursed the dying man. She could not and she did not argue with him, but she revealed to him a redeemed, Christlike life. Love was in her face, tenderness was in her touch, grace was on her lips, peace and joy in Jesus radiated from her, and lo! that which encyclopedic knowledge that puffeth up, and vast learning, and brilliant argument, and eloquent speech had failed to do, this humble, inspired life did. He was converted and died in the faith.

An infidel challenged a man of God to debate about religion. "I accept your challenge on this condition," replied the man of God, "that I bring 100 men with me to testify what faith in Christ has done for them, and you bring 100 men to testify what atheism has done for them." The challenger was nonplussed, withdrew the challenge, and there was no debate.

Meek and lowly, but glad and bold witnesses, who witness by lip and life and shining look, are the strongest, the unanswerable proof of the inspiration of the Book by which they live. The final proof will be given when the risen Jesus appears with crowns and thrones and kingdoms, honor, glory, and immortality for those who have believed and loved and followed Him to the end, and opens the dark gates of doom and banishes into "indignation and wrath, tribulation and anguish every soul of man that doeth evil."

THE POWER OF THE NAME

By Edward Joy

From "The Old Corps"

Reprinted by
Salvationist Publishing and Supplies
London (1975)
First published (1944)

When temptations round you gather,
Breathe that Holy Name in prayer.

I have told this story again and again in one place and
another, and I should never forgive myself if it were not
on record here. Maybe some other stumbler toward liberty
may hear in it the truth that God's mercy is full of
forbearance, and that the most despairing need not lose
hope.

This tale concerns one who had been a drunkard for
more years than I can remember. His name was a byword
among us for all that was wretched in sin. He was the
bogey of the children--filthy, bleared, seared; not very old
as time goes, but decrepit as if years had passed over his
head. He crawled around begging a drink from any who
would "treat" him. His most-used nickname was that of
"Tom Swilltub," acquired because of his habit of sopping
up the dregs other men left in their glasses. His coming
into any respectable public house--you understand what I
mean by that adjective--was the signal for a howl of
protest; only in the houses of the lower order was he
barely tolerated.

One day he listened in the street to the Gospel
message as told by the Army. Nobody thought he was
listening, for he crouched by the door of a "pub," waiting
for opening-time as if in a drunken slumber; but he was,
for all that, even though too lazy to open his eyes. I have
often wondered what particular word or song penetrated
his muddled brain, but the Sword of the Spirit has a
mighty thrust, and that day it pierced "even to the
dividing asunder of joint and marrow." He heard the word
of the Lord and woke to righteousness. He came along to
the meeting, stumbled out to the Penitent Form, and
sobbingly poured out the tale of his sins. Some of the
lookers-on thought his tears were drunken and maudlin,
but, as a matter of fact, they were of a "sorrow meet for
repentance."

Then there began a fight such as Tom thought he
would never win. He went from the Penitent Form toward
his home, but before he reached there he was in drink
again. He came back to the Penitent Form. Again he
went to the drink; and once more he came to the Penitent

Form. He came and went so often that little wonder we grew skeptical about him.

One day new officers came. The little wife was the sweetest, most trustful woman I had ever met. She was, from the first, the idol of Tom's eyes--and she knew it. She returned his slavish affection by the most persistent faith for him. She seemed to say, "Though all forsake thee, yet not I." "I will have faith for him no matter what happens," was her motto concerning him.

So, every time Tom came to the Penitent Form, it was one or the other of them--the Captain or his wife--who accompanied him home. They saw him past the doors of the drinking-places and helped him in a hundred ways. His gratitude to them was pathetic. But he fell again and again.

One Sunday afternoon in particular comes to my memory. We had had such a splendid day. In the morning there had been many "forward to the Table," and the afternoon "Free and Easy" had been a time of glow and glory such as sent us all away in high spirits for the night event. On his way home, his heart full of faith and a song on his lips, the Captain came across Tom lying drunk in the gutter. His faith fell a whole set of points. But he stooped to pick up the bleary drunkard, and once more prayed his dauntless petition, "Lord, send us some way to help him!"

The prayed-for help was delayed, however. Tom fell again and again, and then, as if to take away his only hope, the officers farewelled and Tom was still a drunkard. The next man was stern and full of the judgments of the Lord, and at length he went so far as to forbid Tom coming any more to the Penitent Form. Whereupon there were two schools of opinion among us.

Dear old Mother Dowell! She was one of the loveliest old ladies you might wish to know. I should think the memory of her is in all parts of the Army world. She had been bedridden for months, but her room was the refuge of all the downhearted of the Corps. All who had any sort of trouble or temptation seemed to make a bee-line for her little room. Many a nigh-broken love affair was mended there, as with her hand covering their clasped hands she would seal the renewed betrothals.

Her house stood on high ground overlooking the Channel, with the town outstretching in between. In the immediate foreground was a little garden, in summer redolent with the perfume of flowers and glorified by the singing of birds. How sweetly the recollection of it comes across the years!

Mother Dowell knew of Tom's failure and woefulness, and when she heard of the Captain's *ukase* with regard to the Penitent Form she sent for Tom. Wondering at the honor and, of course, suspecting the reason, he made his way to the sick room.

What a contrast! The thin, pale face, not much less white than her delicately goffered bed-cap and the spotless bed-clothes; the almost seraphic smile of welcome. Tom-- dirty, dishevelled, his drink-laden breath befouling the room. In awe he waited.

"Tom," she said, breaking the silence. "Tom, have you tried the Name?"

"The Name, ma'am? I don't understand you."

"The Name of Jesus, Tom!"

"The Name of Jesus, ma'am? Do you think that would help?"

"Yes, Tom, that would help."

He stood there by the bedside, looking out toward the sea. "The Name of Jesus? How would that help me?"

The old saint reached out her hand and drew his glance to herself:

> "When temptations round you gather,
> Breathe that Holy Name in prayer!

"That's what I mean, Tom. Try that, my man!"

Then Tom understood. He bowed his head, his tears falling fast, for he felt his utter hopelessness and helplessness. "Jesus!" he said, "help me!"

Dear saintly Mother Dowell said, "Amen!"

Thenceforward Tom tried the Name. He said it over and over to himself as he went down the hill into the town. "Jesus! Jesus!" It came to his lips as he hesitated on the threshold of the first public-house he came to, and--strange, passing strange to him--it carried the day. "...and devils fell...." The days went along, and still he continued his prayer. What a fight he had, but every time, the Name conquered. Whether he craved for a drink, or whether it was a passing thought, he said, "Jesus!" Oh, glory be to the Name!

The days passed; they lengthened into months and years. The chains were loosened, the fetters falling, and Tom went forth and followed. He had discovered the power of Jesus' Name. Again and again he said it, constantly it was on his lips; even when he was feeling no particular temptation he breathed the Holy Name in prayer for the mere delight of it. Tom marched with us as a recognized Salvationist, and, I think, the town gloried with us.

One morning he stood on the main street engaged in a business conversation just by the door of a public-house. A stream of men passed in and out, and the constantly opening doors of the saloon wafted the fumes to the street, as if they were the very breath of Hell. What impulse was it that made Tom turn into the saloon and walk up to the bar and call for a drink? He failed to see the evil grin with which the barman greeted his request. I wonder if he was quite conscious of what he said and did. Thirstily, impatiently he drummed on the counter, all the fiends of Hell rejoicing in their apparently easy victory. A moment fraught with all the possibilities of tragedy!

At the back of the bar was the sitting-room of the publican's wife. A trim little room, always cozy and neat, a direct contrast to the smoky, sawdusted saloon. The wife must have had some drawings to religion--or was it the Watchful Spirit who had so planned it?--for on the wall of the parlor, facing the open doorway, hung a text:

J-E-S-U-S!
THAT IN ALL THINGS HE MIGHT HAVE PRE-EMINENCE.

The drink was at Tom's elbow; nay, more, the pot was in his hand; but he was staring fascinated, not at the drink, but at the text--the Name! Jesus! Jesus!

The Name conquered. Spilling the liquid on the saw-dusted floor, taking no heed of the barman's demands for payment, he rushed from the place and into the street as though he had been the man running from the City of Destruction. Saved by the power of Jesus' Name!

The years rolled on. Tom was no longer known as "Swilltub." Some who came to the town, ignorant of his story, wondered at and thought it blasphemy that across his Army guernsey was blazoned the Name: "Jesus." They soon heard the story, however, for Tom was always telling it, and we gloried in it the more we listened. Not so long ago I stood on the spot where his final deliverance was wrought, and wished that a brass plate might have marked the site.

One evening Tom lay dying. The sun of the lovely spring day was setting across the Western Bay, its last lingering glory flooding the room in which he lay, lighting up the text-card which was ever before him. He was going home to be with God. During recent days all those who came to see him had been asked to sing of Jesus, and now, this last evening of his life, they had been singing the verses of "Jesus, the Name high over all." His hand slowly beat time to the singing, and when they came to the last verse it dropped lifelessly beside him. He gave one last slow smile and was in the Presence.

Happy if with my latest breath
I may but gasp His Name!